12-95

By the same author
Inside Dance

MURRAY LOUIS
ON DANCE

a cappella books

a cappella books
an imprint of Chicago Review Press, Incorporated

Editorial offices:
PO Box 380
Pennington, NJ 08534

Business/Sales offices:
814 N. Franklin St.
Chicago, IL 60610

Front cover photo: Murray Louis in *Index* (1973)
Photograph by Tom Caravaglia
Endpapers: Murray Louis in *Odyssey* (1960)
Photographs by David Berlin
All photos courtesy of ProArts International, Incorporated

Library of Congress Cataloging-in-Publication Data

Louis, Murray.
    Murray Louis on dance.
        p.   cm.

    ISBN 1-55652-147-2   : $19.95
    1. Louis, Murray.   2. Dancers—United States—Biography.
I. Title.
GV1785.L68A3   1992
792.8′028′092—dc20
    [B]   92-6468
                                                            CIP

To Mama, who had faith in the beginning
To Fran, who took her place
And to Nik, who never doubted it

Contents

Introduction 1
Essie 7
Why Do They Do It? 15
Sex and Sexuality 23
Distinction 31
Command Performance 39
Childhood 45
Diary of a Bum Knee 51
Immortality 63
On Death 69
The Inner Person 73
The Grand Manner 79
Benefactors 85
Bucks 97
Speed 107
Change 113
Rehearsals 119
Dressing Rooms 127
Makeup and Costumes 133
Performance 141
The Curtain Falls 149
Conclusions 155
Notes to Myself 159

Foreword

MY FIRST ENCOUNTER with Murray Louis came in 1976, when he invited me to see the choreography for his new dance *Glances*. He asked if I would be interested in writing the music for it—a task I willingly accepted but one that began a process that posed many difficulties for me. While watching a videotape of the completed choreography, I tried to compose music that synchronized melodic and rhythmic ideas with the existing movement. Happily, Murray seemed to like the results, and *Glances* is still in his repertory, danced to music arranged and recorded by my son Darius.

A few years later, our next collaboration, *Four Brubeck Pieces*, reversed the process. Murray choreographed to *my* pre-existing music. For live performances with my Quartet, we had set beginnings and endings, and a known number of bars, but 90 percent of the music was improvised each night. Murray's choreography reflected this freedom, and every night the finale exploded with high energy. His young dancers took off like jazz soloists, improvising on movements from the established choreography, expressing the core of their beings in a dance that allowed them to say, "This is me!"

The risk-taking involved in the creation of *Four Brubeck Pieces* resulted in a sublime union of movement and music. While fully exercising our individual creative freedom, we recognized and respected the disciplines of our respective art forms. Clive Barnes summed up this successful collaboration in the headline for his review of the work published in the New York *Post:* The dance was a "perfect blending of two art forms."

Murray Louis has written "on dance," but the thoughts he presents cover a wider range—from his own particular perceptions gained from years of experience as a choreographer-dancer to an overview of all art. Murray understands the joys and the heartbreaks of a committed, creative life. *On Dance* offers an intimate, sympathetic, and frequently humorous look at how artists prepare, cope with, and sustain their art. Murray offers introspective musings on immortality and death as well as illuminating insights into the personalities—dancers, benefactors, impresarios—who have shaped the course of American dance history. It is a wide-ranging book that has helped me to understand better the workings of Murray's complex, creative mind.

If I were to suggest an alternative title to this book, it would be *On Survival*. Survival in both life and art is the book's overriding theme. *On Dance* is applicable not only to dance and dancers, but to all art and artists.

Dave Brubeck
April 1992

Odyssey (1960). David Berlin

Introduction

I'VE NEVER THOUGHT OF dance as being part of my life. I've always known it as my entire life. With that overwhelming commitment, it is understandable how all of my values and perceptions have always emanated from a dance compulsion.

Some of my earliest childhood memories are about dance. My mother was a young girl when she arrived in this country. She arrived from the heart of Europe, and I don't believe she ever learned the English language with any fluency. I was six at the height of the Great Depression, and totally ignorant of the desperate financial plight of one-third of the nation. I had seen Shirley Temple in the films and was determined to learn to tap dance. I must have cajoled my mother into investigating a dance school. Where it was located or exactly when this all took place I cannot remember. I do recall walking up a long, narrow flight of stairs, holding onto her hand. I do remember going to an open door and seeing dozens of little Shirleys, curls bobbing, hoofing their little hearts out. I remember my mother taking my hand and leading me out and down the stairs and trying to explain to me that we couldn't afford the price. I don't remember my reaction, but I do recall the tuition was twenty-five cents a lesson. A fortune.

I never waited to be taught or waited to be supported in my creative efforts. I just did it.

She died shortly after that. For many reasons I wish she had lived

1

longer. She must have loved me dearly to walk up those stairs, and it must have pained her severely to walk down.

I never took lessons until I was twenty. I did my own thing—I danced. Although I danced continuously, even choreographed, I did it because it was the most natural thing for me to do.

Born dancers never question their destiny, although on occasion some of their paths seem to lead them through what seems like purgatory. Fortunately, they are blessed with the gift of seeing the light at the end of the thorny trails.

Through my forty-five-year career as a dancer, choreographer, and teacher, I have crossed paths with the whole gamut of the dance world. It often broke my heart to see so many dancers, with that life-strong determination of a salmon, bucking the tides to go up the stream against all odds. But that is what this profession is all about, highs and lows. Glory and heartbreak. Confusion and answers.

I suppose I could call myself "a natural-born dancer," because, before I was twenty, I was self-taught, which meant doing what came naturally. I also had an innate sense of structuring movement and made up my own pure movement dances. I jitterbugged, folk danced, ballroom danced, tapped; I just danced. It took me fifteen years to earn, as a concert dancer, what I made dancing in night-clubs before I began my training.

In thinking back, I realize what gave form to my first dances was my keen sense of movement dynamics and rhythmic innovation, both of which stemmed from my urgent need to move.

One day as I lay on my back stretching, I began to wonder, "How many times have I done these stretches?" Easily a million times, I thought. But as I began to calculate, it came to about 15,000. The sum came as a shock. Why did it seem so much more? I had thought the figure would be in the millions, and the facts showed it in the thousands.

"Simple," my logic explained. "People judge their lives by single years. Dancers judge their lives by seasons. For a dancer, there are four seasons to a year. A season is based on work opportunities: home season, foreign and national touring, summer festivals, and rehearsals. These all carve out their appointed times. Dancers gear themselves differently for all of them."

In a sense, a dancer's life can be gauged at four years to a normal year. So that after a twenty-year career, a dancer has lived eighty years. That's a lot of living. That's a very full life. Several lifetimes, as a matter of fact. If each decade is lived to the fullest, each period has a clear beginning and end, in retrospect, of course.

For any artist such as myself, there is much to be thankful for in this accumulative life. Backing up the art experiences are numerous living experiences. Influences are accrued from every direction.

I did not pick my heroes. Various men and women have, through their exceptional gifts, imprinted themselves on my ethics of life and art. They are a most incongruous lot and make very strange bedfellows. Indeed, I wonder what Beethoven and the Blue Meanie have in common. Nevertheless, portraits of both hang near my desk.

And then there is nature. The sun, the sky, open fields, my garden, all reminding me of their gifts. The greatest gift nature has given me is to assure me to take heart, that there is always another season to come, that I must live in the future as well as the present. The gifts are surprising and come in all shapes. I remember the vivid shock of rejuvenation as I unwittingly came upon the newly born deer near a thicket, or the helpless frustration as I watched a blue jay destroy a nest, or the surprised pleasure of a rhododendron finally blooming after years of surly leaf growth. Or the blood-red sunset over the Hudson River that terrified me with its apocalyptic vision.

There is also the mindless sanity of the mundane. Classes, calluses, and coffee.

I suppose an identity does emerge from all this, but that is for others to say.

What I do know and appreciate now is how complex the identity of an artist is, especially a creative artist. How concurrently run the multiple inner identities of an artist-performer, and that, however inflexible a mind-set might be, it will change as events around the individual inevitably also change. True, there are constants, but they are taken for granted because they comprise an artist's skills, and an artist never stops at skill.

Ten years have passed since I wrote *Inside Dance,* an earlier collection of essays, first published in *Dance Magazine.* I wrote then for the readers of that magazine. With this collection I wrote, in a sense, for myself. It is part story, part journal, part specific, part mystical, but all focused on understanding the intensely personal nature of the art. Time is involuntary, like breathing, and consequently passes just as unnoticeably. Change is inevitable. This collection is about how the artist changes within and about how his art changes without.

Journal (1957). David Berlin

Essie

I KNEW I WAS going to be late the moment I woke up. I knew I was going to be late the moment I got out of bed. I knew I was going to be late at breakfast when everyone forgot to make the coffee. I knew I was going to be late when, getting dressed, I remembered I'd left the shoes I was going to take with me in the country.

Everything that morning shouted "late," and what's more, I didn't give a shit because I didn't want this engagement to begin with.

I hated traveling abroad. I hated the indignity of customs, of work papers, of search, of suspicion. Ever since that inspector in London asked why I wore my wristwatch on my right arm, I've never been able to trust my answering remarks. But forty minutes in their back room and a thorough search helped curb my wise-assed answers.

Laden with two bags, a shoulder pouch, and the wrong jacket, I raced to a cab waiting at the corner. I made it before the light changed. Piling into the cab I gave the driver the address. He patiently turned his head and said, "Sorry, I'm on call and waiting for someone."

Getting out of the cab was not as easy as getting into it. Eight minutes later, I flagged another cab. After settling down, I told the cabbie, "La Guardia Airport."

"Sorry, I've got a slow leak in a back tire. This cab will never

7

make it to La Guardia." Getting out wasn't as difficult this time. I was already practiced.

A third cab pulled up. Was it OK if he dropped the lady sitting next to him at 96th Street first?

This one was easy because I didn't get in.

And then I saw Essie. She was standing across the street waiting for the light to change. She was deep in thought and didn't seem to see anything around her. She was staring into the oncoming traffic and for a moment I almost forgot my urgency. She looked drawn, and her hair looked stringy and orange. She still possessed her commanding bosom and held herself well, but somehow she looked wispy.

A cab drew up one inch from me. He could make it to La Guardia, and so could his cab. But none of that mattered any longer. I turned and watched Essie as she crossed the street.

She looked in my direction, and I quickly turned my back and got into the cab. I did not want to talk to her. It was nothing personal, but her memory was too poignant. She had innocently taught me something painful, something I'd never forgotten. So I did my best to avoid her look and any chance of her seeing me.

Once inside I thought, "That was a lousy thing to do. I should have talked to her or at least said 'hello.' " It was too late to stop, to turn back, but it didn't matter, the rest of the day belonged to Essie.

I first saw Essie dance in concert at the Henry Street Playhouse. She looked wild and lusty, and I was taken by her immediately. She used music I'd never heard before, and she moved fearlessly. I didn't understand what she was doing but I understood the doing itself. She herself danced with great conviction, and she strongly motivated her small company of dancers. There was a rawness about the whole evening, "a sweet disorder" about everything, as if things were formulating just then, and this gave the program an immediacy and excitement.

Essie danced very well that evening, and all in all, I was impressed and carried along with her. What more could any artist ask from his or her audience?

One summer, many years later, Alwin Nikolais taught a summer dance session in Europe. I went along as his assistant. Maurice Béjart was also on the staff. One day the head of the school came to Nik and said, "There's a young lady here from America. Her name is Essie Parker and she says she knows you. She would like to give a concert tonight for the students. Should we do this?"

I could see Nik grow uncomfortable. Making judgments of other people's work is always awkward.

Neither of us had seen Essie dance in five years, and Nik explained he was not familiar with her recent work. The director would have to make her own decision.

That afternoon a concert was announced for the evening to be performed by an American dancer of the avant-garde persuasion. At the concert I sat in the front row with Nik on one side and Béjart on the other.

The curtain rose on a stage empty except for a little hand-cranked portable phonograph in the downstage corner. A young lady placed the needle on a record and left the stage. A garble of words came from the little speaker. At first the language was totally unidentifiable. I thought it was Russian and paid no further attention to it.

Then Essie appeared. She had gained some weight since I'd last seen her, and she wore a white leotard and tights. A sheer pink scarf rested across her ample bosom. She danced with an indulgent romanticism as if in response to the talking. With a shock I realized the record was a reading of W. H. Auden or e. e. cummings, so distorted it sounded like gibberish. Béjart turned his head and looked at me for some clue as to what was going on. I did not return his look.

The dance ended and there was applause.

Another record was put on, the player cranked up again, and Essie returned, still in white, but now a blue veil enveloped her bosom. I could sense the puzzlement of the audience grow. It was one minute into the dance when audible titters from the audience began. Béjart looked at me again, and I held my focus steadily forward and bit my lip. Nik sat staring forward stoically. The titters became louder, and the second dance ended.

Once more the phonograph was prepared, and once more Essie appeared. But this time the titters turned to laughter, and the laughter lost its amusement and became derisive. Suddenly, like a splash of ice water, Essie ran from the stage and the curtain closed. It wasn't funny any longer. Essie had been laughed off the stage. The audience rose, thinking this was the end of the performance. Some applause began and sounded even crueler as it trailed off.

I turned to Nik, who sat quietly staring at the curtain.

"What shall we do?" I asked.

"Someone must go to her," he replied. "You stay out here and get things going at the reception. I'll go back and see her."

When Nik reappeared I asked, "What happened? How was she?"

"She's all right," he assured me.

"What happened?"

"When I got backstage," he began, "she was at her dressing table crying."

"What did you say to her?"

"I asked her if she had learned anything."

"Nik," she said, "I've been laughed off the stage before, but I have to do this. I just must perform. Sometimes it actually works. But whether it does or doesn't, I must do it."

"OK," he said, "now get yourself together, get dressed, and come upstairs to your reception. That's something else you must do."

In a few minutes, Essie appeared. She entered as another guest rather than as a triumphant performer. She saw it through admirably. Soon she was holding court surrounded by her audience. She looked radiant and at ease.

What I learned from all this was how fierce the need to perform could be. I took the experience a step further and realized that professionalism and artistry were two separate things. There were artists who were not professional, who suffered because of that, and there were professionals who were not artists and would never be great, however saleable their work might be. But the combination of professional and artist was surefire. Obviously this was the happiest combination, the artist who knew how to present the work. Once I made this distinction, I was able to look at and see performances with a better understanding of intent and achievement.

But somehow I could never get out of my head that need. "I've been laughed off the stage before, but I must do it." Do what? Why is it so necessary to court humiliation?

I learned why during a long career of dance, and so have all performers. The Orientals call it "losing face." What artist at some time in a career has not been laughed off the stage of his or her own ambitions? Humiliation is inevitable in this profession, and dancers must prepare to face it sometimes in their careers. The heights they reach in performances need to be descended from carefully. Humiliation waits for one false step.

10

There is a hemp mat that lies outdoors on the terrace of my apartment in New York City. The floor of the terrace is cement, and the flowers grow in boxes filled with earth. This is how gardens grow in the cities, in the crevices of civilization, window boxes. Hanging a few feet from the mat is a bird feeder. Now, laymen know that birds chirp, but bird-watchers know birds also spit. Not saliva, but seeds as well as shells.

By the middle of summer, the little hemp mat turns into a miniature field. The need to grow, "to do it," is so strong in nature that any seed landing on that mat takes root. It doesn't matter to that seed that the soil and situation is all wrong, that it is doomed. It has to do it.

Not too long afterwards, Nik was coming out of a subway station in New York City and met Essie.

"Nik," she said, "you're just the person I wanted to see. I know you've appeared uptown," she bubbled on, "and I've been thinking about doing a Broadway season this year and wanted to ask you about it. Tell me about prices and what theater would you suggest and . . ."

Well, what can I say?

The need is indomitable.

It is in the order of life that certain horses must race against the wind. They must hurl their huge bodies parallel to the ground: legs extended, tail flying, and nostrils flaring into space.

It is in their genes that certain animals must stretch to their fullest, must defy gravity, must tear the cocoon of complacency. All of which make them troublesome and disturbing members of their society. But there is no other answer for their behavior other than that they must do it.

Twenty years later I told this story to a class I was teaching. A woman, a visiting dance teacher from Switzerland, was in the room.

"Oh yes," she said, "I remember that concert. I remember how strange it was. It was so funny."

"Then it was true," I thought. Time hadn't clouded my memory. But why, I wondered, with all the comic-tragic episodes I'd lived through, should I remember that one so clearly?

"Tell me," I asked her, "was it as I said? Did you remember it as I had?"

"Oh yes," she said. "She was the first American dancer I'd ever

11

seen dance. I thought she was so foolish. Whatever happened to her?"

I got up, excused myself, and left the room. What had happened to Essie wasn't important now, it was what had happened to me because of her that mattered.

I couldn't face the thought again. "I've been laughed off the stage before, Nik, but I just have to do it." I couldn't face the thought that I, too, had to do it. Would I someday be laughed off the stage? Is that a prospect we all face?

Great dancers are considerably ahead of the Essies and those mat-prone seeds. They know why they do it. Oh, perhaps not in so many words, but they know, and more important, they also know how to do it.

Improvised Solo (1955). David Berlin

Why Do They Do It?

"WHY DO THEY DO IT?" and indeed, what do artists get from this extreme output? Money and fame? The twin seducers of the id and the ego? Surely there are other rewards for their excruciating commitment? And there are, but they are difficult to talk about or put into words.

When people ask dancers why they do these things, the answers do not come easily. They hedge, they stumble over definitions, they grope for meanings, yet they know what they want to say. They have answered the question to themselves many times. They are hesitant to talk to others about their reasons. If they say, "I enjoy it," it seems too trivial and dilettantish. To say, "Because I do it better than anyone else" is far too arrogant. That "I have something to say to the world" is too imposing. Dilettantism, egotism, and arrogance are uncomfortable ways to justify a life in art. And since no one cares to be portrayed by these motivations, much less make them public, dancers avoid moralization and deal with the question more realistically by doing it. They let their performance answer the questions for them.

When dancers lie in bed after a performance, legs throbbing, muscles so sore that the slightest shift in position warrants the most painful effort, knowing there will be only four hours of sleep this night before they must be in the lobby checked out and ready to leave before the sun is up, they wonder. Sinking into a too-soft mattress without the will or strength to get up and put the mattress

15

on the floor before the strain settles into the lower back, uneasy because of an inadequate performance that night, helpless to defend themselves against the insidious breeze of an uncontrollable air-conditioning system, stomach rumbling because of a too-late dinner, they ask, "Why do I do this?"

They also ask it after endless hours of rambling and pointless rehearsals. They ask it at unsuccessful auditions. They ask it as they put on their makeup and realize another year has passed.

They ask and answer these questions endlessly and go on to the next ones.

"Why do they do it?" First and above all, there is the physical pleasure of movement and the ecstasy and exhilaration it brings. To become as one with the flesh, the soul, the universe, the unknown, is the dancer's reason for being. There is a release and intake of the spirit in every pore. It is a communion, it is the partaking of glory. It is an intoxication of the muscles. This physical pleasure comes through the lungs in the exhilaration of exhaustion, through the pores in the radiance of sweat, through the instep in the passion of stretching. It comes with the expansion of the body to encompass the space around it. It comes with listening to the eloquence of silence as the next gesture awaits its cue. Oh, they know why they do it, they know. But how to say it?

And they do it for money. That is, of course, when they can get it. And they do it for fame, which sometimes outlasts them, and for prestige.

Knowing you're getting well paid does make the task easier. You feel your work is respected and valued. If there is no other reward for the output, at least there is money. I remember one gala program of stars at which I appeared. Two dancers came offstage. "There," one said, "that will pay for the new fireplace." Immediately everyone in the wings laughed, because somewhere in the back of everyone's mind, that engagement was also paying for something they needed.

They also do it to prove themselves. Some urged themselves on this way in the beginning of their careers. Some because it is, happily, the thing they enjoy doing most. Some do it because they can do it brilliantly. Some feel they have been chosen by fate to pursue this course and will not disturb the inevitability of their lives. But to the layperson, the reward hardly seems to compensate for the racking and sometimes tawdry price the dancer must pay.

16

Many years ago, during my nightclub dancing days, I shared the only dressing room in the club with all the other performers. There were six of us, and the prettiest of all was Georgiana. In fact, she was a ravishing beauty. Everything about her was special: her arms, her wonderful body, her perfect legs, and her red hair. She was also a fine dancer. She could do anything. At that time, I had never seen anyone with so great a range of movement. She was billed as an exotic dancer, which usually meant lots of writhing on the floor, backbends, and acrobatics. One day as we were preparing for the show she said, "Sometimes when I dance, my ankles feel so sexy." She giggled when she said it because she couldn't explain what she meant. Of course, the rest of us in the room thought that wasn't all this kid was probably into, and grew uncomfortable and embarrassed. But today I know perfectly well what she meant. Sexy? Ecstasy? How often have those words traced across the mind of a ballerina *en pointe?* How often have her insteps brushed those words?

Ecstasy is an abandonment of the senses to where the muscles have led them.

"Why do they do it?" They do it for this ecstatic feedback, which they, in turn, feed back to the audience.

Dancers' lives are confined. They are trapped by their intense devotion to their art and the sensitivity of their nerve endings. They are bound and made love to by their muscles, and seduced by the passionate muse. The voices of reality that belong to the world around them have a hard time getting through to them. They don't seem to hear when one asks them, "What will you do when you stop dancing?"

Dancers have their own way of seeing the future. It is either the opportunities tomorrow may bring, or the final immortality. There is very little in between.

No one in his or her right mind thinks that dancing is a lucrative, long-lasting, or secure profession. Certainly the motivations rest elsewhere. Certainly its rewards rest elsewhere.

The European opera-house policies regarding pension plans and retirement differ wildly from the freelance insecurity of the American dancer. Yet both benefit from their circumstances and both suffer. Why do dancers ignore their economic future? Because at the age they begin and achieve their skill, they're not concerned with it. They are invulnerable, young, glorious, beautiful, infallible, and success is theirs.

The length of a dancer's career is limited. The physical intensity of the profession places not only a strain upon the body, but upon the psyche as well. But whereas the body eventually shows the strain, the psyche can rejuvenate itself and grow stronger and wiser with time. The power of the mind will always outlast the prowess of the muscles.

Dancers, as a rule, start early and train during their teens, arriving at the starting line at twenty and finishing at forty. Of course, there are many exceptions to this timetable.

There are three major periods during a dancer's development when the question arises as to whether this profession is appropriate: the initial commitment; the period of training; and the final mastery of the art.

The decision begins with the initial commitment. This occurs anywhere between the ages of eight and twelve years old. True, any adult would gasp at this preadolescent age of consent, but then again, to anyone who knows children, these years are a curiously mature period of human development. The period before biological sexual awakening and rapid body growth is a remarkably calm one. A stage of similar rationality and balance is not reached again for many, many years. Unhampered decisions made during this period can be trusted to a large degree.

The next eight or ten years are the period of training. It is also the major weeding-out period. This is when the commitment is severely challenged. The physical output is backbreaking, the emotional instability crippling, the psychological barrage unbalancing. During this period, the dance teacher must emphasize to young dancers the degree of commitment the profession will demand of them. A career cannot be based wholly upon starry eyes. During this period of singular focus and spartan bleakness, 85 percent of the aspirants drop out.

By the age of eighteen or twenty, with substantial technical development at their command, dancers should be fairly directed in knowing where and with whom they would like to dance. By twenty-three, their careers should be reasonably assured, or as assured as anyone can be about any career in the arts. If they should change their minds at this time, there is still the opportunity to change and redirect themselves. There is still time to undertake another profession.

Because dancing is not a lucrative profession and has a limited

18

income-producing period, nature has wisely arranged for it to occur at a time in life when people are least concerned with middle-age security: at a time when youth is inured against injury, unconcerned with acquisition, when the word "age" has not, as yet, become a part of their vocabulary, and before they have their feet caught in the glue of economic responsibility.

To understand dancers, one must think of the life span as a division of the early years, the middle years, and the later years. Some people arrange their lives to make their statement during their middle life. Others live for their early years when their physical prowess is obviously at its height.

Tulips bloom in the spring, chrysanthemums blossom in the fall; that is their timetable. Dancers bloom early, presidents bloom late.

When I was teaching children, I vividly remember arriving at the realization that there were young children and old children. This gave me cause to consider seriously the Eastern concept of the soul returning many times, each time one life older than the last. Perhaps dancers are a breed of first-lifers.

Time is one of the life forces one cannot coerce or rush. No one knows this enigma called time. Indeed, it has no identity. It wears many disguises. To become discernible, it must be felt.

Time is also very quiet. It can slip into the corner of a life and not be heard from for many years, especially when that life hurtles rapidly along. Then suddenly it will rise and stretch its limbs, and your life will stop for a long-overdue accounting of itself.

Most of us know time physically by the strain that waiting places on us. Few of us have the time to notice it as it tumbles along in the guise of heady opportunity.

Dancers have a very particular response to the passage of time. Their thinking is clearly concerned with the current moment; the future is unimportant, at least, not as important as the present. It is a decision that says, "Why should one waste the present to prepare for the future?"

For dancers, the importance of their art rests in the doing.

There is no right or wrong in the many ways people deal with the present and the future. Dancers give their life and energy to the beginning of their lives. Others spend their lives planning for retirement.

"Tell me, what do you expect to do after you're through dancing?"

This is the question asked by those people who have no idea that achievement exists for some people at the beginning of their lives rather than at the end. During the professional years, the question does not become relevant until the specter of injury and illness makes the relevance both seen and felt.

During the twenty years of a professional career, unless dancers take proper care, they will also be left by the wayside facing the problem of what to do when they can no longer dance.

To maintain any degree of longevity, a dancer must take care of the body. Even if the head is screwed up, the spinal column must be aligned.

Maintaining a career reasonably free from injury and sickness is of great concern to a dancer. Massage, chiropractors, ice packs, acupuncture, and hot water are a very ready part of most dancers' daily treatments. Tight muscles, pinched nerves, misalignment, and general fatigue are the Four Horsemen of the dance. They spread panic, injury, depression, and doubt.

Professional dancers respect their physical equipment. Some dancers are blessed with easy facility while others must pound themselves into flexibility. But it cancels itself out. Those with stretch have to work for strength, and those with strength must work to lengthen their muscles.

Because of their extraordinary circulation and muscle tone, dancers rarely look their age, which is another reason it appears that many retire so young.

As a rule, in the ballet particularly, men retire from the stage before women do. The physical demands of jumping are the major contributors to this. The punishment to the knees, hips, and ankles is devastating, and the toll it takes, alarming. Sometimes dancers seem to push themselves deliberately to encourage an injury so that they can leave the field of battle honorably, wounded in action.

But for those who fulfill their performing careers, there are multiple areas to engage in afterwards. The first are those directly related to the profession itself: teaching, coaching, administration, and creative direction. Closely related to these are careers in the other medium: directing, TV, stage, and films. There is also the academic network in universities and colleges. Careers available outside the profession generally are creative ones, or those that deal with the public.

In any case, can anyone imagine beautiful or handsome, energetic, talented, vital, and alive people having difficulty extending their careers?

Generally, professional dancers develop a business sense during their careers. Their heads come down from the clouds long enough to look at their bank accounts. They begin to use the income earned in their peak years wisely. Generally, I said, because I know a dozen dancers who cannot read a bank balance, whose arithmetic is limited solely to counting beats.

Then there are the "stars." Almost all of them today have business managers who, hopefully, invest their clients' incomes wisely. The marketing value of a "big" name also has potential earning power long past the years of performing.

And then there are the great artists who, by the manner in which they lead, direct, and shape their careers, set standards for newcomers. Their dignity, grace, intelligence, and ability to handle their careers in early life and their roles in later years bring assurance, and dispel a great deal of fear about a full life after they can no longer dance.

The only real sadness of retirement from the stage is to know there is no other occupation in the world that can possibly bring you up to those heights, back to the gods, as only the dance can. This, whether you realize it or not, is the real tragedy of the early-lifers, the dancers.

They must now wait for the spring to awaken them and bring them to life, when once their blood was quickened by every performance.

Chimera (1966). Max Waldman

Sex and Sexuality

ALL THOSE WHO ATTEND a dance performance find themselves at some point during the evening undressing the dancers with their eyes. Why not? Long limbs, luscious rounded muscles, firm buttocks, and pert breasts. Dancers are usually young, attractive, healthy, strong, vital, and often are as exposed on stage as is allowed by law.

Physical attractions are considered by everyone. Regardless of what choreographers say, somewhere in the back of their minds they consider their dancers' sex appeal before casting them. It is essential that the audience identify with the dancers. What better way to guarantee this than through an empathetic seduction? Pliant torsos glistening with sweat, bold and assertive, taut and alive, the dancers cut across the stage daring you to possess them.

The time boundaries of a performance are always foremost in the mind of the choreographer. The immediate contact with the audience is imperative, be it an opening theatrical effect, a striking initial movement phrase, an unexpected entrance; all these devices are considered. But what can guarantee more instant attention than an attractive body?

If beauty lies in the eye of the beholder, so does sex appeal. Sex appeal directs itself along two paths, the sensual line and the erotic bulge. The sensual is insinuating, the erotic is blunt. The sensual leads to a long-lingering pleasure, whereas the erotic strikes hard and fast. It victimizes and consumes with overwhelming blatancy, trammeling all formalities. Desire supersedes all reason.

The floodgates strain and the storm descends. The vessel barely rides the storm. It is all a matter of staying afloat, staying alive. No one is immune to Eros's arrows. More than one career began with an erogenous tingle in a critic's loins.

Sexual bents have clouded many a scruple. The power of the pelvis is formidable. When passions are aroused, superlatives flow. The erogenous targets are all too tempting. Cupid's arrows may be careless, but they are also humbling. In the private world of viewing, they shamelessly reduce sense to sensuality.

Great performers are generally not known for their sex appeal, primarily because they never let it dominate their art. That restraint is a very important discipline. However, they know the potency of their sex appeal, and use it as a backup rather than an up-front device. They will employ sensuality primarily because its generous and subtle range can considerably enhance their poetry of motion, their art.

Dancers are an amazingly varied lot. They come in two sexes, all ages, and many lifestyles. Their motivations give them singular distinctions. It is difficult to generalize about dancers' sexual proclivities because they demonstrate them differently according to their age and style of dancing (i.e., modern, ballet, jazz) and, above all, by what originally motivated them to become performers.

If someone were to analyze the physical appearance of a dozen great dancers, they would be amazed at the divergences and strangeness of physical proportion; the short or overlong leg, the various-sized bosoms, the different line and curve of buttocks, the thickness or thinness of torso, the muscularity of chest, arms, and thighs—from virile to androgynous, from nubile to luscious. In the hands of an artist, differences and shortcomings become blessings.

Sexuality doesn't give itself away at first glance. It is dealt out slowly throughout an evening, until it has entered the viewer's perceptions as subtly and carefully as has the art.

Onstage, there are both calculated and innocent seductions. The erotic focus of an audience is manifold. When wantonness is intended, the lascivious eye will roam and drink. When there is innocence in performance, the concealed eye, enjoying Susanna at her bath, relishes the sight knowing that the performer is unaware of the exuded sexuality, which is doubly titillating. Does a harbinger know its awakening power? Do those who herald and invite listen to their own song? And if they do, are they aware of the tingling chord they strike?

✗ The more obvious technical erotic tricks reveal a certain degree of calculation. Pelvic action, facial "come-ons," cleavage, and quivering breasts are parts of the prelude to the oldest profession. The power of the innocent performance, however, is that the performer is not conscious of lustful observation, is unaware that someone in the audience is watching and not viewing the performance intended for them to see, but is instead clearly absorbed with the performer's body. Here is a private moment of union, and from this union comes fantasies, and from fantasies come fans.

One of the headier spices of performance is the flavor of eroticism. The overuse of these erotic spices can engulf a serious performing intent. Chefs must be careful how they season and release pungency. Carelessly used spice calls attention solely to itself, distorting and dominating the flavor of the dish. As any good chef knows, a pinch of strong stuff is sometimes essential, but can also go a long way. The same is true in performing.

Dancers are synonymous with sensuality because their physical appearance bespeaks a sexual health. Radiating through sweat-flushed pores, a glowing skin sings with health. As with Venus when she arose from the sea, the water, lending a sheen to her skin, revealed an allure that has forever bespoken desire.

Everyone has his or her own preferences regarding the sex act. The intent, practice, skill, and pleasure are all personal gratifications. Passivity, dominance, seduction, and aggression all come into play. From revulsion to exhilaration, from abandonment to terror, from cruelty to tenderness, even the practice of foreplay and post-caring differ. No two are alike in their formula for sex, and each engagement will differ. Nothing can be repeated in the same way. Professional purveyors of sex come close to guaranteeing a standard for their services, and even they are constantly challenged.

Up close, physical attractions center about the head, neck, and hair; but from the distance of the stage, the torso, breasts, genitals, buttocks, and legs take precedence.

Every guy in every dressing room, be it athletic or theatrical, looks to see the size of every newcomer's penis. It's an instinct. It's a ritual. It's a sign of admission to the tribe, as well as a sign of comparison. Men are more at ease with each other after they have seen one another in the nude.

What disturbs some men is their fear of latent homosexuality, like some people have a fear of latent maturity. Men confuse affection towards other men with homosexuality. Men also think looking at other men in the nude is evidence of homosexuality. Homosexuality is the active engagement in sexual activity between people of the same sex. If there has been no participation in this sexual preference, there is no homosexuality involved.

All over the world, in dozens of cultures, boys and men often walk embracing each other, or hand-in-hand. They like each other. They are comfortable feeling each other's physical contact. It offers security and a communion without words, a statement of affection, of confidence, of trust.

In the dance profession, homosexuality is as common as is this nonsexual male companionship. No one makes a big thing of either. Dancers are both gay and straight, and there is rarely any strain between them. They comfortably use each other's sex-slang vocabulary. They don't challenge each other.

Homosexuality is a condition of sexual preference; heterosexuality is a condition of sexual preference.

If pleasure from sexual union were the only criterion of social acceptance, then one could compare the two. They both can fulfill that objective. If companionship and love were the only factors, again they both could fulfill themselves.

In the late 1960s, the youth revolution created havoc with society and carved major inroads into the existing social morality. One of the important results of this was the relaxing of attitudes regarding the body and its exposure. This led to a great relaxation of sexual mores. Modesty ceased to be an active verb.

The effect of this revolution on social dancing was overwhelming. The pelvic region had its day. Rock dancing brought everyone onto the dance floor. Alone and unencumbered by the formality and patterns of partnered dancing, the dance floor became an erotic playground. Social dancers could direct their pelvic thrust to a partner or a group of partners, or fornicate the space around them, alone.

The fashions in clothing that accompanied this new abandon were equally revealing. Cleavage and crotch prevailed. The body was no longer restricted by jackets and skirts. People were allowed to view the human body in less shadowy terms. Their eye could relax and see more, could cut through the first veil of embarrassment, overcome the guilt that came with voyeurism, and accept the exposure of the body, accept the total body as an instrument of dance and of the excitement it provoked.

This new attitude helped popularize the dance with large, new audiences, and allowed choreographers a vital new freedom in designing new movement. In earlier times, nothing other than a dance belt hugged a dancer more tightly than did his or her modesty. People dressed carefully by themselves in the most secluded corners of the dressing room. Certainly no one entered the others' changing rooms.

Today, smaller dance studios have only one communal dressing room. Dressing together has imposed a physical familiarity with the opposite sex. All the usually covered parts are not only exposed, but arrayed so that they can be compared. Pretty heady stuff for a young lady or man. But inhibitions are quickly overcome—large penis, small penis, full-breasted or flat, pubic hair—this is what you've got and this is who you are. Welcome. Now let's get on with rehearsal.

In my day, dating was an unbelievable agony for teenagers. What you expected and what was expected of you were debilitating pressures. It wasn't until I was in the Navy that I could look at the body of a nude woman or man with comfort and pleasure. Today, if you're curious, you look. If you're interested, you can touch.

Speaking for myself, I enjoy the human body. I hug, embrace, and kiss everyone. In class, I don't hesitate to maneuver and manipulate misplaced pelvic regions and upper thighs. The dancer knows the difference between passion and placement, the difference between the pelvis and private parts. In teaching class, hips, thighs, knees, arches, lower spines, chests, heads, and necks all need alignment. I roam through class pushing and pulling. I don't find this erotic in class, but in bed it's a different story.

Dancers often find themselves in the role of partner or of being partnered. This is when a great deal of erotic awkwardness develops between boys and girls. They often have to hold the most intimate positions during rehearsals. If they fall out of character and into the realization that this is the Kama Sutra position number six, they are done for. The role they are playing, whether abstract or narrative, serves as a desensitizer when bodies are wrapped around each other. But the slightest letting go of that role, and those sensors go right to the crotch.

27

Choreographers are careful to maintain that fine line between erotic and gross: angling the body so that awkward ass transitions are facing upstage and seeing that crotch exposures don't interfere with the continuity of a phrase. A great deal of this editing is left to the dancers, who are often the better judges of where their weight placement is, to minimalize any erotic blatancy.

The performers are constantly aware that the audience is focused as much upon their private parts as they are upon the head, arms, and legs. Therefore, before they leave the dressing room, there is that little extra attention given to the grooming of these parts.

Dancers spend long hours together. Their after-work circle of friends generally consists of dancers as well. New members of companies are immediately evaluated as to whether they are available or not. The working-dancers' hours make meeting new people difficult. Convenience is the name of one of Cupid's arrows.

But not all dancers find this exposure an inevitable step towards consummation. On the contrary, there is a strong belief that the energy needed for dancing can be drained and dissipated by sex, that semen is also seminal to performance. There are strict self-imposed limitations dancers adhere to, especially during performing seasons.

However, rehearsals don't seem to draw from the same source. Rehearsals don't demand that extra push that performance does. Abstinence is not necessary now. No matter how brilliantly a rehearsal may go, the dancer does not push into the cell linings and abdominal wall, as is done during performance. That extra thrust can be used for other pleasures.

When dancers complain about being tired, they do so from a standing position, but once prone, when their legs no longer have to hold their weight, it's a different story. The dancers' legs, particularly the strength in the thighs, are a constant concern. Anything that might drain their force is to be avoided. The whole debate as to which enervates and leadens the legs more, red or white wine, is argued constantly. The same goes for sex.

It is very often not the passion in dancers' hearts that governs their sex life, it is the strength in their legs.

Entre-Acte (1959). Sosenko

Distinction

WHO ARE THESE PEOPLE, these luminaries we call performers? Most people recognize them from their appearance onstage. Few know them without their theatrical light. Their glowing centers radiate outwards in bands of blinding brilliance, catching up all who pass their orbit and searing them. They brand their viewers and forever lay claim to them.

What makes them distinctive? They bear little resemblance to each other. They think differently, they behave differently. They think both the best and the worst of each other. They are not alike in most aspects of their lives. Yet when they prepare for and appear in their art, similarities do begin to emerge.

Distinction comes in all sizes and attitudes. It appears in the mature and immature, in the generous and self-centered. Distinction is being one's identifiable self. What makes distinctive artists special is the effect they have, as performers, upon the viewer.

There was a time when a strong national or ethnic flavor gave one an unusual and exotic appeal, but today there are few national boundaries. A self-conscious embarrassment of national ego has replaced patriotism. It is safe to say, though, that geographical and social climates do spawn special aesthetic sensibilities. The soil for the cultivation of modern dance was more suitable in the United States than in other countries, and the story ballet was more acclimated to the European temperament.

The genetic traits of every performer help shape his or her distinction.

There is no norm, no average for distinction. It sits alone at the extreme ends of the scale. It is good, good or bad, bad but rarely in between.

The American nature is an eclectic one. Because of its complicated cross-breeding, it has no singular ideology and in this way differs intrinsically from European elitism. Elitism belongs to a linear heritage, a singular cultural development upon which sits an aristocratic crown. America by its very nature is multiheaded and wears many hats.

Performing stars are distinctive, artists are distinctive. They draw attention to themselves and to the companies with which they appear. They can fill houses and generally do so, and set their fees accordingly.

They are champions. They know how to race and know how to win. They are distinct by their professional standards and by the recognition they've gained. They move easily through the international performing scene knowing what is expected of them and delivering it. The two things most of them know best are their profession and themselves, and consequently they talk of little else.

Distinction also makes physical demands. These performers are no longer on the stage for two minutes of glory. As professional artists, they must sustain whole evenings.

Some are godless and some devout, but they all share one common belief: their devotion to performance. They know their value, although they must confirm it to themselves continuously. They know the courage that lifts them fearlessly into the air. They know the ecstasy of pushing through into the fullness of their art. They are pilots who steer the audience effortlessly through a journey of motion and imagery.

With dancers there also goes, hand-in-hand, a basic formidable technical facility, some of it hard-gained in the studio and some of it a gift at birth. Their technical brilliance is made distinctive by their intelligence, quick memory, timing, endurance, persistence, passion, and a ready wit. In performance, they can cope with almost anything. They are rarely thrown off guard. Their pace, mien, hauteur, and impeccable assurance make them formidable. Timing and command are at their fingertips, but emotionally they are always vulnerable.

32

Their intuitive judgments are vivid and real. They live in a world of mystical and glittering responses. They don these intuitions as easily as they don their tights, but should their assurance be challenged, they become irritable and restless and bear the vitriolic look of a wet cat. Their attentions are always quickly brought to the curiosity of movement and how it feels as well as looks. They have an appetite for movement that they must nourish.

They also contain within themselves the seed of disturbance. Whereas people in general seek to create a balance in their lives, performers have an essential disruptive factor buried deep inside that instinctively denies constancy. This antibalance hormone pushes everything to risk level. It is the fuel for their volatility. It creates the gasp of breath taking, the constriction of the held breath.

There are also dangers in gaining distinction. It can imply prominence in only one area of performance. It is easy to become typed and gain a reputation for specialities, as is often the case.

For the young and new arrivals to the scene, exploitation and opportunism are additional pitfalls; as in nature, there are certain fruits (like strawberries) that when plucked too early don't continue to ripen but instead rot. The same can be said generally for performers and artists. There is a premium in being vine-ripened.

Pride, among other things, plays an important part in distinction. It sets personal standards and also helps to keep one's back straight.

Distinction is easily recognized; achieving it is another matter.

As performers grow, they slowly clear the underbrush in the tangle of their personalities, but they never tamper with the center they contain, the core about which their lives revolve. Through the art experience, they recognize this center; with the art participation, they strengthen it.

This center is the most important source of dancers' confidence, strength, balance, security, and power. They nurse and protect it. If it is shaken or jeopardized, their performance is doomed. It is their Achilles' heel. Artists keenly feel this center because they feed from it, and it is also the basis of their physical setup.

Dance superstars are a recent phenomenon. Earlier dance stars were called divine and legendary, but with the combination of mass audiences, excessive media hype, and high finances, a new luminary has appeared, the superstar. From the beginning of the history of personalities, politics and notoriety have played a strong role in establishing recognition and fame. Bold headlines have always spoken louder than discreet critiques buried in the bowels of a newspaper. The combination of a great artist and international political involvement is definitely front-page material.

Rudolf Nureyev's spectacular artistry and equally exciting defection from Russia catapulted him into a household word. Mikhail Baryshnikov and Natalia Makarova had the same thrust into stardom. But despite their escalation, they kept their feet firmly based on their brilliant artistry and were able to ride their sudden and dizzying takeoffs. Biblical Salomé may very well have been the greatest dance artist of her day, but her reputation today is pretty much based on her political activism.

The audiences who came to see Isadora Duncan, I'm sure, were at first strongly motivated to buy their tickets to see this scandalous "naked" woman dance. After a while, Isadora used her headlines for her own advantage, but in time she did become a victim of her press. Her marriages, her lovers, her career, the tragic deaths that surrounded her, and her political involvements were all flamboyant, and were further inflamed by the media. Fortunately, it is her artistry that remains with us today.

The difficulty with superhype is that it feeds upon itself. It has brought very large audiences into the theater, and with the economics of today's productions, costly as they are, it is necessary to keep this large attendance flowing. The major question that arises is one of aesthetics. Does the audience come to see artistry or the headline, and should the management care as long as it fills the houses? After all, why else do managers retain a battery of press-relations people and advertise so heavily?

Artists do not create their reputations, that is done by others. Artists create art, others sell and distribute it. Once the artist is on sale for public consumption, that public must be dealt with as consumers, and the process of packaging begins.

Every art can claim its masterpieces. They are the achievements and composites of skill, beauty, and aesthetic resolutions. Indeed, the more masterpieces an art contains, the more confident and substantial does that art become. No art form pins its reputation on any one masterpiece or any one artist. Great performers are masterpieces. They represent the diversity of the art, and the art gains its distinction by the intensity and artistry of their distinction.

Some of these artists are at the mercy of this dance compulsion with which they have been born. They yearn for the life of complacent conformity but, helplessly, must follow their genetic calling. They rebel, they withdraw, they run, they bemoan, but to no avail. They have been chosen.

Sanity can jeopardize distinction. The rational dancer stands a strong chance of being overlooked. This is because of the nature of the viewer. Eccentricity has always enjoyed a full house, from Bedlam to Barnum.

Contrary to some thinking, I feel the artist is a mutant creature in whom nature has planted a deviating strain from the common denominator or norm. I suppose madmen can also claim this distinction, but they never quite get their acts together.

Artists train not so much to be artists but to survive as distinguished ones.

Styles are the social garments worn by periods of time. Styles also identify the various vocabularies within an art. Dancers come to these movement styles because their nature and physical compatibility favor one over the other. There are tap dancers, ethnic and modern dancers, gymnasts, ice skaters, swimmers, and social and ballet dancers, all of whom train their bodies differently.

Gradually these dancers elevate themselves by their acquired range of movement onto another plane of sentient refinement. The body, with its new abilities of extension, speed, strength, and flexibility, charges the nervous system to behave more keenly. Their perceptions become acute and finely honed.

To understand dancers, one has to realize their susceptibility to imbalance. The extremes they undertake make it difficult for the physical and the psyche to operate together with any regularity. The nervous system, never made to bear stress well, often finds itself victimized by the breathtaking physical achievements of a superb dancing body; the body is a startling technical facility at the mercy of a capricious nervous system.

Dancers are artificially bred and, once out of their very carefully controlled hothouse climate, may easily fall apart.

Their lives today take them to a great many environments they cannot control. Some situations are common to everyone, but many are unique to this profession. To know dancers, one must know how they cope with the specific world to which they must relate.

Although the stage is the scene of their achievement, their testing ground also includes airports, buses, dressing rooms, hotels, rehearsal rooms, stifling heat, air-conditioning, and cement floors. All of these are as much a part of dancers' portraits as any great technical feat they may perform.

In addition to their strong techniques, they develop strong ambitions, strong wills, and with these come strong doubts. Fears are not always negative. They are part of the body's protective mechanism. They are alarm systems. They warn of the future, of the challenges still ahead as the eye stretches to the next horizon.

The events dancers encounter, from the trivial to the momentous, reveal a complex patchwork. Their daily lives are filled with a barrage of images, places, people, and gossip. Rumors are the lifeblood of gossip. Unfounded as most rumors are, dancers nevertheless feed on them and find them necessary stimulants, all of which both divert and influence them.

Dancers can look at motion as if through a telescope. They can investigate movement from its broadest base and then reverse the lens and penetrate deeper into themselves to inspect the most minute motional sensation. The nervous system reacts to stimuli and texture. Muscles respond to effort. It is at this primal level that the body of a dancer communicates with the body of the onlooker. It is at this depth of innerness that art first stirs.

Dancers roam this internal sentient land. It is their center. Their attachment to this inner landscape is never severed. It is home, and throughout their careers they will return there many times to refresh, revitalize, and nurse themselves. It is here they visit before they step onstage, and here they return to when they can no longer bear the harsh reality of the profession.

What all dancers have in common is the instrument with which they will practice art to uncover sensation. They all share this common nomenclature, the human body.

Dancers begin their careers with this natural gift, the body, and then through a long process of unnatural shaping and devising, gain the means to craft and perform a vocabulary of movement.

This intense concentration of exaggerated training is for the most part a distortion of the body's capabilities. Forcing the legs into a rotated or turned-out position, or deep *pliés* in first position, are not advised by orthopedists. The pressure on the knees and arches does not bode well for middle-year adjustment. But curiously, through this severe and unnatural physical discipline, they are able to penetrate deeper into the meaning of motion.

Dancers' lifespans differ from their career spans. The first is a reasonably guaranteed event. The other hangs on a thread, a thread chewed upon by chancy opportunity, heavy competition, and limited recognition. Recognition comes in all degrees: hordes of fans at the stage door, people stopping you on the street, autograph requests in a restaurant, or seeing your name in print. What's in a name? Everything, especially when it is yours.

Anyone who's climbed the heights is a star, which makes for a crowded firmament. But, on a clear, moonless, autumn night every name is up there and visible: some glowing brighter than others, some gathered in clusters, and some standing nobly alone.

The brightest jewels are not always set in the crowns that they deserve.

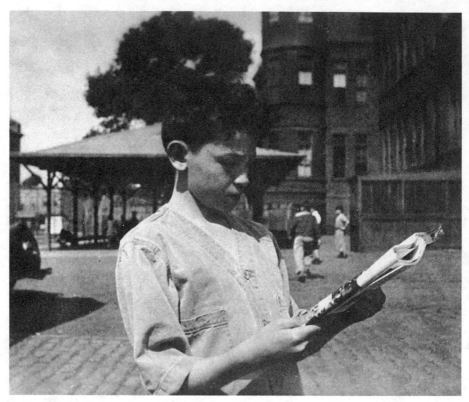

At the Orphanage

Command Performance

THE HAPPIEST DAYS OF my childhood were spent in an orphanage. Unfortunately, the longest hours of my life were also spent there.

In the years 1938 to 1942, Brooklyn was a beautiful suburb of Manhattan. Quiet, obedient, sleepy, open fields, and trees, all of which barely exist today. It was a time of trust and personal security, of virginity and neckties. Public schools were taken very seriously, and teachers were treated with great respect. Going to the films was taken as an occasion for dressing up. Movie stars were not taken lightly. You did not bring performers into your home, as we do today with TV. You dressed and went out to the picture palaces to rendezvous and pay homage.

The building that housed the orphanage was designed as a huge palace, with many rooms, and hundreds of children. The orphanage was located on a very large tract of land that included ballfields, playgrounds, a large wooden infirmary, three pavilions, a small brick nursery for infants, and, of course, the enormously imposing turreted palace itself.

Adjoining the sweeping main-entry staircase was the library, lulled by the steady ticking of a beautiful old grandfather clock. The room was L-shaped and contained several thousand volumes. If in my time there I did not read every book, I at least handled each one. There being no librarian to maintain any order, the children took it upon themselves to keep a semblance of some organization.

There were classrooms, living rooms, music rooms, indoor gymnasiums, huge dining rooms, dormitories, two laundries, workshops, playrooms, kitchens, nurseries, two candy stores, auditoriums, and on and on. The place was a fantasyland for any child such as myself who liked to roam and discover, read and be alone.

During the daytime, we dressed in street clothes to go to the school outside the orphanage. After school, we changed into a comfortable overall in which to play and be messy in our own playground. We had daily chores and a schedule, but once these were fulfilled, our time was our own.

One hot August day, my little clique of cohorts decided not to further humiliate ourselves on the baseball field (we had just lost a game the day before, 82–0). We did not have a pitcher. In fact, none of us could throw a ball that could reach home base, and we'd walked about eighty of those runs. After the initial frustration, we took to laughing until we were all lying on the ground, doubled over at our futility. The game lasted six hours, and the truth was that no one would play against us today. As we sat in the East Pavilion discussing life and Tarzan, the sound of shrieking sirens filled the air. Every child was alert, and suddenly the day had a purpose. To the right of the tall open gates, smoke rose over a row of low two-family houses.

To the cave dwellers, fire meant heat, protection, and palatable food. To the Romans, it meant hot water. To the insurance companies, bankruptcy, and to the child, fascination. The lot of us raced off as one to follow a long, red, splendid hook-and-ladder engine, which careened, screaming, around the corner.

It was the lumberyard. That sprawling woodpile was ablaze. A large crowd was already in attendance when we arrived, watching the production of lights, radios, police cars, policemen, strings of hose, fire engines, ladders, water, barking dogs, traffic tie-ups, shiny helmets, fire, and smoke.

From the distance, a long whining siren drew closer and closer. A black car drew up and the police surrounded it. The door opened, and the mayor heaved out. It was really him, it was La Guardia, the father of New York City.

Everyone cheered. We were saved. Like the Lone Ranger on flashing Silver; Buck Rogers with ray guns blazing; Tarzan swinging through the jungle; the "Little Flower," donning a fire hat, charged forward to put out the fire singlehanded.

Oh how we cheered, for if ever New York had a hero, a Lochinvar, a Robin Hood, a headliner, it was this short, round, shining symbol of integrity and virtue: Fiorello La Guardia.

Of course he extinguished the fire with one hand, brought order to the snarled traffic with the other. Disbursed the dogs. Waved to the folks and saluted the children. Oh how we laughed and cheered.

We walked home, slowly preparing our story to ensure as lethal a jealous reaction as possible from the other kids on the ballfield who had missed the fire. Oh, what a wonderful afternoon. Imagine, the mayor.

That fall I was in the sixth grade. Mrs. Vogel was my teacher. She was truly extraordinary. At milk-and-cookie time, she encouraged us to bring apples as well, and as we all watched breathlessly, she would split an apple cleanly in half with her bare hands. Then the poor slobbering lot of us would also try it. But carnage was all we produced. Torn skins, mashed pulps, and dripping sap covered our hands, laps, and desks.

That season someone on the board of education had created a toy library. Instead of only books, children could now borrow different toys from the library. The idea was a great success. To celebrate the project, our school was going to prepare a pageant. It was no secret that I could dance, and Mrs. Vogel volunteered me for the program. Together with a little dark-eyed girl, I was to do a pantomime and a waltz.

The pantomime was staged to the "Wedding of the Painted Doll," and the waltz to "Puncinello, the Clown." I had not realized how elaborate the production was to be until I was given a costume that fit. Rehearsals were never a problem for my partner and me because we both enjoyed dancing, but the ducks in the Mother Goose scene gave everyone a bad time. Those ducks just couldn't remember anything.

We opened in early November for three performances. On the opening night everything went well; my hat did not fall off. After our waltz the applause was resounding. We bowed and exited. But in the wings there was a great deal of buzzing, and finally Mrs. Vogel came to us and told us to go and dance the waltz again. After we left the stage, Mrs. Vogel said, "Do you know who is in the audience?" We both shook our heads. "The mayor. Mayor La Guardia is here and liked you so much, he wanted to see you dance again."

So there. If not a command performance, at least a command encore. A triumph. And that was not all: Mrs. Vogel split an apple and gave us each half.

Oh, yes. Fifty years later in Los Angeles, while having dinner, a recording came over the air of the same Puncinello waltz. I stopped eating and listened. I remembered that earlier event and decided to dance to the music again. The new solo was to be called *The Disenchantment of Pierrot*. Fifty years and a whole lifetime had passed. The world had changed beyond description for me. I looked about the posh dining room, I reviewed my life, and just about everything had changed, except for one thing: I still couldn't split an apple.

At the Museum of Natural History

Childhood

WHEN NEW YORK WEARS its autumn crisp and tangy branches crack the sky, then a boy such as I, delighting in every opportunity to be morose and misunderstood, finds refuge from a world that arrogantly insists upon going its own way by running off and hiding where no one can find him. To run off and into the only arms that understand and embrace him. For me, this place was the city, my city. Here I could sing all my songs, play all my roles, and the most thrilling of these parts was: myself.

I remember the first time I ever saw a picture talk. Not a film or a motion picture, but a painting. I was sixteen, I believe, and as was my custom in those strange and unfathomable years of growing up, I often spent the cold, clear winter Sundays at one of my second homes, the Frick Museum.

The museum, housed in a mansion that the millionaire had built for himself, partly to keep up with the Morgans and partly to house his art collection, is situated on Fifth Avenue and overlooks Central Park. Duveen, the art dealer, was assigned the enviable task of assembling an art collection worthy of the income of an American industrial baron. But for some reason, at the end of this impressive financial outlay, when the house and furnishings were completed and assembled, Mr. Frick never lived in the house to enjoy its truly overwhelming splendors. But I did.

After entering the museum, you passed through the atrium with its heady earthy aroma of languishing leaves, through the circular room with Whistler's elegant linear ladies, into the long gallery. This was my favorite room, this gallery. Here I sat, together with Rembrandt and Raphael, on many a blue-lit winter afternoon.

It was on such a day, as I sat alone, staring at a Rembrandt portrait, that the head in the painting turned, looked directly at me, paused for a moment, said questioningly, "Yes?" and then turned back.

Well, what can I say? Every hair on my head stood straight up. My eyes opened and froze. My breathing stopped. Had this been the films, a choir of angel voices would surely have filled the room, and the Red Sea would have parted again.

To an impressionable romantic sixteen-year-old, the effect was shattering. When my breath returned I looked about me. I was alone. I was here on 70th Street in New York City, but for a moment I was suspended in time. Had I joined the 17th century? Or had it joined me? A picture had talked to me. What did it mean? For a moment those eyes had caused a rent in the canvas, and I had stepped through.

I could never be the same, nor was I, ever. It was as if a mighty key had unlocked every door, and I could now spend my life opening them. Nothing was closed to me now, but then again nothing was open, only unlocked.

I looked at the painting again, desperately trying to regain the attention of those eyes, but of course it was futile. When the moment has passed, there is only memory. Rembrandt had cut through three centuries to speak to me. Rembrandt.

At this early stage the performer is already being formed. The lines of antiquity to the anxious present are firmed and secured. Recall and memory flow easily and quickly, detouring occasionally to include the many oblique impressions that will eventually lend pungent character to the individual.

There are times when the nature of an impression is frightening and alarming. Fright works in two directions. Left to itself, it can immobilize and inhibit, but pushed further it can become a catalyst to a remarkable range of noble conclusions.

The ability to be awed, stretched by fright, and melted by anticipation. Eyes forced apart by wonder, sealed tight by anticipation. Possessed by the strength of imagery. To be so awed, to be so taken that the imprint presses itself into the cell to become part of the organism. A vertical impression is incised, not a shallow horizontal scan.

When one considers how fragile is the aesthetic world, how a musician is allowed to enter the world of music only through the touch of a fingertip, details count.

I never asked advice from children. Advice is based on experience. What experience can a child possibly have, except perhaps in fear? I looked to them, though, to see the process of intuition. As containers of innocence and inexperience, they make clear flacons in which to observe the intuitive process. If they are still unclouded by patterns, their translucency makes them excellent scientific controls in determining the undefinable.

Through the veneers of maturity, you must keep open that path to childhood, where you knew the oneness of innocence and cruelty, the sweet tears and the bitter ones, where fate and fact drew blood. You must remain open to that place where all is bathed in that eternal elixir, hope.

As the child grows, its input continues. New data of sight, sound, and sensation are added to what has already been programmed. Light brings visibility, but the blinding sun is too fierce for eyes developed in sheltered darkness for nine months. Only at sunset when it has cooled its passion can mortal eyes look upon it. However, for frail mortal eyes, for those who cannot look at the sun, there is always fire and its consoling flame.

Long expanses of sea, air, and earth tune the mind to the inner frequencies, but fire, that great poultice, drawing the heat from feverish eyes, sears a special path into the inner person.

Flames bear a special fascination for young people. Candlelight is not overwhelmed with romantic implications as it so often is with older people. It is mysterious and beckoning, dreamy and compelling. The promise of faith is lit by candles, and hell can only be envisioned properly by torchlight.

Treacherous paths are treacherously lit by fire. The journey inward is managed with great trembling. The inhabitants of the interior are reflected by flames. This is not a safe place. What if the fire should go out? There would be darkness and all the fear that goes with it.

Superstition should not be treated lightly. It is one of the more powerful explanations of God.

The memories, the lore, the experiences of the past have been passed along, stored, and programmed into the receptacles of the genetic structure. Each cell is a repository of the atavistic past and the antic present. The memory banks are filled, stuffed with the gorgeous garbage of sensation, with the peels and shells of undigested living. Images appear from nowhere and are unrelated, like undated and forgotten postcards.

The journey of limbs and love is always in earnest. Sensations are stored, memories stuffed hastily in corners of the mind to be relived when they are called upon, aired out in the present.

Soon, however, passion rears itself with puberty. The gamy beast stakes out its domain, urinating its intoxications on every pleasure, making every new sensation no longer a moment of childhood, but of lust.

How long can the gates of childhood remain unsealed? And is it safe to go forward if we leave them unguarded? This leaves us with only one recourse, to grow both forward and inward. How is this managed? To grow forward at one time in life and inward at another? Or both simultaneously? Or ignore one in favor of the other?

The portion of childhood that has been lived mustn't be lost in favor of contemporary distractions, because the juiciest fabrics of the imagination were woven in those years, and all later conclusions will reverberate from these innocent springboards.

Personae (1972)

Diary of a Bum Knee

IN 1983, I APPEARED in Tokyo in a gala performance together with some of the most extraordinary stars of the international ballet world, performing *Déjà Vu*, a solo for which I had received much acclaim. For the preceding year my right knee had been troubling me, and I could do nothing about it.

I had gone to masseurs and chiropractors, doctors and witch doctors, all of whom gave me advice and attention, but the knee continued to swell. During that year I had continued to ice it heavily to lessen the swelling. I applied every ingredient anyone recommended, but what was more worrisome was not knowing what was wrong.

I had not fallen on it or hit it. I had not wrenched or snapped it. I had never heard anything tear as I had with my other injuries, and what was more confusing, the swelling would go from one knee to the other. Obviously this was because I would favor the injured knee.

What should have been a wonderful two-week season in Tokyo turned into a painful regimen of icing, resting, and preparing my leg for each performance. The simple matter of walking became a nightmare, and the very thought of turning barefoot on that rosin-saturated floor would bring tears to my eyes.

At the final performance, as I raised my leg in the finale of the piece, I looked at the swelling that had occurred during that performance and told myself that this was it. When I returned to

51

New York, I would have the knee operated on. The sleepless nights, not being able to find a comfortable resting place for my leg, and the insistent throbbing in the knee had by now taken away every pleasure of dancing. This was in August. I had no commitment until the fall.

In New York I stopped every physical activity and rested the leg. But I was not prepared to end my dancing career so suddenly. I had not left a will. I had not left a testament of my career as a dancer.

I went to see Howard Klein, who was then with the Rockefeller Foundation, and told him of my plight. I told him I wanted to film twenty of my solos before I retired. Some years before, Howard had helped fund a very successful film series I had made for dance in colleges and schools. He agreed and came through with half of the funds to start the project.

The worst thing I could have done for that knee was to rehearse dances my body was no longer familiar with, because rehearsals cause more damage to the body than performances. But I went ahead with it.

I switched legs for certain difficult steps and marked a great deal, all the while icing and resting, icing and resting. The studio, cameramen, and lighting were all arranged, and the shooting began.

I don't think I ever lived through a more agonizing two weeks. The more difficult dances were done in one full-out straight shoot. After that I dropped to the floor, where I remained until I could walk off the stage area. The stress on my body was enormous; by the end of the filming my cheeks had sunk, and no amount of makeup could disguise the darkened hollows. To add to the nightmare, several important dances had to be reshot because the cameraman had framed too closely, and the figure had no breadth or space around it.

I watched the rushes and felt there was enough of everything to indicate what the dance might have been had I not been so crippled. Now it was really time to say good-bye to my dancing career, and I went about in earnest to find the best surgeon for the operation.

I had always felt that if I could not dance to the standard I had set for myself, I would stop dancing, sorrowful as the prospect was.

I talked to everyone I knew who had been operated upon and the consensus was Dr. X. He had performed hip, cartilage, and meniscus operations, and so I went to see him. He was authoritative and confident, and my first job was to have an arthroscopy of the knee to determine what we were specifically after.

As I lay on the X-ray table during the arthroscopy having my leg twisted excruciatingly, and easing my pain with loud screams and groans (which could be heard throughout the waiting room), I could feel the injected fluid sloshing around my knee. Then suddenly the technician said, "There it is, there's the tear." It was my meniscus and they had it there in print.

The prints were sent to Dr. X, and I went home making embarrassing farting noises with my knee, stopping walking when I felt people staring at me.

We talked on the phone about the operation. It would be surgery, then three months (with luck) in a cast, then three months of therapy, and I'd be walking comfortably again (walking, not dancing).

We set the date for the operation. His nurse called the day before to verify the operation. She had to know definitely by 5:00 that afternoon to reserve the operating room and the anesthesiologist. Yes, I said I would call her later.

I don't know what I did. I think I sat down and stared, and then the phone rang. It was Andrew Bales, my manager. I had completely forgotten that Andy was in the hospital having another futile operation on his hip. He was under sedatives, but he had to tell me of a new operation that was being performed that didn't cut the leg, and he wanted me to do nothing until I investigated it. He couldn't go into detail because he was dropping into sleep. I believe it was he who mentioned Tommy Tune. So I called Tommy Tune, who said, "Murray—it's remarkable what they are doing today. I went into the doctor's office and he operated right there and I walked out."

Unfortunately his doctor was on vacation, and I had to give an answer by 5:00. It was now 1:30. Could he recommend anyone else who did this operation? Tommy could not think of anyone else. I thanked him and hung up.

"You need a doctor to do microsurgery?" a voice said. It was the air-conditioner man who had come to make a repair. He had overheard the conversation.

"What is microsurgery?" I asked him.

"Let me show you," he said, and he raised his trouser leg and

53

showed me the barely discernible incisions. "I had my knee done about six months ago."

"Can you bend?"

"No problem," as he bounced up and down in a deep *plié.*

"Who did it?"

"Dr. Hamilton."

"Do you have his number?"

"It's in the book." He found it and I called.

"Yes," Dr. Hamilton said. "Meniscus is no problem. Do you have X-rays? Bring them in and I can be definite."

"I'll be there as soon as I can."

It was now 2:15 P.M.

I called Dr. X's office and asked his nurse to have them on her desk ready for me. I'd be holding a taxi outside.

Now, I lived in the West Village and Dr. X was on the upper East Side, which in New York traffic could sometimes take as long as a day and a half to cover.

At 3:00 P.M. I was at Dr. X's office.

Dr. Hamilton was on the West Side. At 3:45, I was in his office.

"Yes," he said, looking at the X-rays. "No problem. When do you want the operation?"

At 4:30 I called Dr. X to cancel the operation with him.

"Your leg," he said, "your decision."

The message on Friday morning was to check into Roosevelt Hospital at 1:00 P.M. I'd planned to do a great many things that day, primarily to decide on costumes for two new group dances. Frankie Garcia, costumer extraordinaire, called. He was dying. He sounded it. He'd caught a cold and wondered if we could design the costumes over the phone. I thought maybe he'd like to hear me dance the dances for him over the phone.

"We'll get in touch Monday," I said.

"Where are you going this weekend? To the country?"

"No, to the hospital."

"Well have fun anyway."

I'd never stayed in a hospital before, and as I packed an overnight bag, I wondered what the hell to put in it. Toilet stuff I knew since I spent half my life traveling. I knew I'd be in bed a great deal, which meant pajamas. Pajamas? Where would I find a pair? One of the first things I did when I graduated from high school was to stop wearing them. I went to the lower drawer in the bureau, which houses everything no one knows what to do with, and there, sure enough, was a pajama top. Large, unused, and a price tag still attached. What else does one do in a hospital, I thought? Read and think. I took along two mystery stories and a writing pad. On the way out, I added a bag of peaches.

In the cab I shouted my destination over very loud clarinet music coming from a cassette machine on the driver's seat. He turned the music lower to ask me how I liked the playing. "I'm afraid I wasn't listening," I said. "Listen," he said. He turned the sound up. I listened. It wasn't bad.

"How do you like it?" he asked again.

"Not bad, is that you playing?"

"What difference does it make who's playing. Listen."

He turned it up louder still.

It was improvised and good. Without thinking, I made the mistake of asking him if the clarinet was B flat or bass.

He whirled his head around. "You a musician or something?" he asked.

"No, no," I insisted.

"Listen to this," he said as he put in a new cassette.

"You seem to know something about it. It's 'I'll Remember April,' good, huh? Better than Benny Goodman. That Goodman ain't so hot as all that. Goodman hasn't any mystique. Benny hasn't any ideas. You know what I mean? And them coloreds they just play. They play wrong notes all the time. They've made an art of playing wrong notes. Know what I mean?"

We pulled up to the hospital entrance. He continued as I held the fare out to him. Without taking the money, he looked intently at me. "Who are the greatest musicians in the world? The pianists, the violinists, anybody? The Jews! It's because they've got heart, and training. All day long they're training, training."

"Oi!" I thought, "I really don't need this. I'm going to have my knee cut open and this nut is screaming at me over that loud music."

I stuffed the money into the container and got out. "Keep the change, and turn the music down, you're in a hospital zone."

Inside the hospital everything was very quiet. I was alone. The man at the desk pointed to admissions. The admissions room also had but one attendant in it. I was told to be seated and wait. I picked up a new movie magazine edited by Rona Barrett. There was no one in it I recognized except an old photograph of King Kong.

After a few minutes, a very personable young lady led me to her partitioned office. I delivered to her a check for the extra money my private room entailed. Somehow I anticipated a difficult time after the surgery and I wanted to be alone; also, I often read in the middle of the night and didn't want to disturb anyone.

She urged me to check valuables and I did so. A silver chain from Singapore, and four credit cards. Would I wait again in the next room? I did so. During this pause I salvaged my bag of peaches from my overnight bag, and inspected the damage. One peach had a worm in it. It must have happened in the taxicab.

A pleasant man appeared in a red coat about two inches too large for him and asked me to follow him. I did so. We chatted amicably as we walked through a maze of corridors to an elevator.

In the elevator, an extraordinarily cadaverous elderly gentleman lay in a bed. He was unconscious and returning from surgery. I quickly turned my eyes away from him. I was in a hospital, and during the next few days I turned my eyes away quickly many times.

We were going to X-ray, the man in the red coat said as we left the elevator. I followed behind him clutching my bag and my peaches.

In X-ray, I sat in the waiting room while he and the nurse argued. I browsed through an interesting paperback mystery I hadn't read. I could hear that I wasn't welcome, so I pinched the book and put it in my bag.

"They don't do X-rays on Friday," he said, shaking his head. "Since when don't they do X-rays on Friday?" he asked me. I told him I didn't know. In the elevator on the way to my room, I turned my eyes away again. In the corridor on the eleventh floor, he asked me if I had the admission papers. "What admission papers?"

"Oh," he fretted, "I must have left them in X-ray. What shall I do?"

"You go back and get them," I comforted him. "I'll wait here." I don't know if I added, "Don't get lost."

I stood waiting near the central desk, when finally a nurse looked up and asked me if I was waiting for someone. I gave her my name and told her I was to be admitted.

"Why are you standing there?" she said, looking up from the registry. "You belong in room 1121."

Suddenly three people appeared and I was led to my room.

As we approached one said, "Is the room ready?" The second said, "I'll go see," and did so, and the third said, "Wait here, I'll check." So I stopped.

The one who went ahead appeared from the room and waved to us. "Why are you waiting there? Your room is ready!"

I think that was when I got the other worm in my second peach.

A parade of nurses, aides, and people appeared. One gave me a robe, and the others checked things. I put on my robe and waited until everyone was gone and jumped on the bed. It would be a long time before I jumped on a bed, or anything else for that matter.

I read and by 3:30 I became very hungry. I had missed lunch. I opened the bag of peaches. I discovered the second worm. I ate all the peaches and the worms. Still hungry, stomach rumbling, a bag of peanuts would help. I put on my robe, took some money, and started out in search of peanuts.

"Yes," I promised the desk, "I will not get lost. Yes, I will return immediately. No, I didn't need a wheelchair, no, I didn't need an attendant, yes, I would bring her back a Milky Way. Yes, I remembered where the gift shop was."

When I returned to my room I discovered in my brown paper bag two O'Henry's, chewing gum, two bags of peanuts, and a cheese and cracker snack. I had only asked for peanuts and a Milky Way bar. They had been packed by mistake. "Now that's a gift shop," I thought.

I read. I had my temperature taken, as well as my blood pressure. I waited. A lady came to take my food order. She left three cards: dinner and the following day's breakfast and lunch. I noticed on the top a check place for portion. Medium, small, large. I checked large. What a great idea, I thought. I filled out all the menus with great relish, then I remembered that nothing was to be eaten before the day of the operation. When she returned to collect the menus I reminded her I was not to eat dinner.

"I'll get you a double portion tomorrow," she said, and she left.

Dr. Hamilton came to look and encourage. Saturday morning traveling on a flat bed to the operating room. Wonderful view of ceiling patterns. I'd never traveled horizontally before. I greeted Dr. Hamilton in the operating room.

As I went under the anesthesia I had an enormous sense of relief. I knew that when I woke it would be one thing or another. No longer the question will I dance or not, or pain for the rest of my life.

I awoke suddenly. I was in a postoperating ward. The nurse was looking down at me. The operation was over.

"You were out quite a while," she said. She had no idea how lazy I am and that I could fall asleep anytime I lay down or even sitting up for that matter. That, together with the anesthesia, could keep me out for a week.

As soon as I realized where I was I remembered the operation, and all my sensibilities went directly to the knee. It was bandaged and the pain-killers made it insensitive.

"Take it easy," the nurse said. "Give it a chance to heal." I must have been moving it.

Back in my room. Transferred to my bed and alone, I had the knee all to myself. I had been told I could leave that evening. Still drugged, I couldn't imagine this was possible. And then the pain began. There were only three tiny incisions, but oh God, the pain and the immobility. I could barely bend the knee. What had I done? But more pain-killers remedied the waves of hurt.

With the drugs the nurse asked if I planned to leave that evening. The question was so insane I could only shake my head no and said, "Tomorrow."

The doctor appeared. The operation was a success, but he was not prepared for the quantity of frayed meniscus, and sometime in the future we might take out the rest. It had become a long operation, and he was afraid to keep me on the table any further.

He left. Confused and drugged I fell back to sleep.

I woke to go to the bathroom.

The door was ten feet away from the bed, and the bed was three feet from the floor. I had not as yet bent the knee nor taken any weight on the leg.

I sat on the side of the bed and slowly bent, that is, tried to bend, the knee. It would only go so far. Which was not far enough. I put my good left leg on the floor and stood up. Slowly I straightened the right leg, and cautiously put weight on it. Well, the pain was unbelievable.

How in the world did Tommy walk after that operation, and how was it conceivable that I could leave the hospital that day?

I hopped to the bathroom and then hopped to a chair, taking my

58

weight onto my thighs to sit. Again the pain that felt like a cut nerve. Once seated, I stretched the leg. Then attempted to stand, taking the weight onto the thighs.

I realized I was starting my therapy. I hopped back to the bed and collapsed, exhausted. That little effort had drained me.

When Dr. Hamilton came to see me I insisted I stay until the next day. He said that would be all right. I could not imagine how a week of rest wasn't prescribed after the operation, but no, the thinking of recuperation nouveau was mobility as soon as possible.

The operation involved three half-inch incisions into which three tubes were inserted to reach the problem area. Into one tube went the cutting instrument, the second contained a suction device, and the third a camera device that played the image on a screen that the doctor watched. The doctor did not look at the knee during the operation, but rather at the screen to the side of him.

What caused all of the pain was the jabbing of those tubes into the knee. As for the incisions, only two stitches were necessary to close each of them. None of this was explained to me then, or if it was, I was not conscious enough to understand it.

The rest of that day and that night I floated on a euphoria of pain-killers. I vaguely remember getting up several times to work the knee during the night.

In the morning, Nik arrived to drive me home. Stressed and shaken, I thought everyone was mad to insist I get up and walk out. Armed only with a cane, I left the hospital.

The first nightmare was bending the leg to get it into the car. I was not used to such pain, nor such immobility in my legs.

"We're going to the country," Nik said.

"Now?" I moaned. "Never. I must get home and into bed. I've got to rest."

"OK," he allowed, grandly. "Take a nap and then we'll go."

I had to rest after every effort of bending that knee. The next morning I awoke in Southampton, the one place I truly thought of as home. There I began my own therapy. Exercising in the fresh air and sun. Resting, eating to regain the ten pounds I could scarcely have afforded to lose, reading and sunbathing. For the next three weeks the leg grew stronger. Still, I could not flex or extend it fully. Because of the limited mobility I could see a marked deterioration of the muscle tone in my thigh. I became worried. Perhaps I needed professional therapy with machines or something.

I returned to the city and went to the closest sports medicine center. When I entered, I was greeted warmly by an ex-student. After she explained to me all the things I had taught her, I decided to continue my own program of rehabilitation. Still, I could not stretch that leg fully.

I returned to Dr. Hamilton for a postoperative checkup, and questioned the inability to fully straighten my knee. He cut the stitches and tried to explain that absolute full mobility might not be achieved. I left his office and with my cane limped to the street.

"Nonsense," I thought. "There is something there, inside the knee, that is preventing it from straightening. I can feel it." Thirty-five years of dancing had given me some understanding of my body.

I returned home and got into my favorite position, flat on my back with a book in my hands, and plotted.

The incisions had healed. The stitches were out. The leg felt stronger. I could take weight on it. What was holding it back? And then I had it. Lesions. Obviously these three openings had left scar tissue. I had to break those tissues before they grew any thicker.

I got off that bed. Warmed up the knee. Rotating and flexing it, I then sank into a one-legged *plié* with all my weight on it, and "thump," I broke the lesions.

Nothing I could remember was so joyous as that moment when I could fully extend my knee and feel the blood and muscular continuity flow through the leg. The ecstasy of stretching the back of the knee into the Achilles tendon can only be realized once that pleasure is denied. Now I could bring the strength back to the calf and thigh muscles, and then back to dancing.

Not only did I get back to warmups, I got back to choreographing. I hadn't thought much about the upcoming season. All of my attention had been focused on my no longer dancing. With my legs back, it was business as usual. Eight weeks after the operation I was dancing full out at City Center in *Frail Demons*.

Two years afterwards, I had the left knee operated on. I was careful this time to build up my calf and thigh muscles until the day of the operation, and also prepared to break the resulting lesions. It was twelve weeks afterwards that I joined the company in Taiwan to continue the Far East tour.

Eighteen months afterwards I had the second operation on the right knee to finish off what still remained to be trimmed.

With the old "cut" surgery, the entire meniscus or a substantial

60

part of it is usually removed. But with microsurgery only what is damaged is removed, leaving the knee pretty much intact.

Truly some divine hand stood by me that fateful day to keep me from making the wrong decision, from taking the wrong path.

Oh yes—while I was in the hospital after the first operation, flowers arrived; they were from the air-conditioner man.

Junk Dances (1968). Max Waldman

Immortality

SO MUCH IS WRITTEN about dancers as physical people, about their outward appearance, and about the world they live in. But for any artist-performer and choreographer-creator, there is an existence that runs simultaneously with the physical. It's an existence with its own logic, its own continuity, and above all, its own rationale. It's an existence that makes sense only in its own disjointed way. It almost doesn't seem to be housed in the brain but exists in the senses. It's a disturbing intuition that children, madmen, and artists possess. It is called the "sixth sense," and it cannot be explained or understood. It is called "intuition" that seems to be above reason. Ephemeral, yet present, its existence is attested to but rarely trusted. To describe it seems impossible, yet it colors every descriptive phrase. It seems to speak from an echo chamber, hollow sounding, unreal, yet so crushing when it bears down with an opinion or illusion. It is often not taken seriously because it cannot be explained. But it visited me once in the beginning of my career. I suppressed it then and have never let it come that close to me again.

It was during a performance of *Journal*. In the last dance, which was a philosophical resolution of the suite, I found myself totally in possession of the movement. My body was almost moving by itself when suddenly an inner voice said, "Levitate." My consciousness and concentration were shocked by the intrusion, but my body continued.

"Go ahead. Levitate. Take off."

The panic created by the voice and its urging would have driven anyone to stop and freeze, but the dance continued.

"When you get to the next arm lift, rise."

"No!" shouted another voice. "If you take off, you might enter another dimension and never return."

"Here it comes. Get ready."

"No. Don't do it. Don't listen."

And all the while I could feel myself get lighter and lighter.

The moment came. My toes gripped the floor. I did battle and weathered the crisis. I forced myself to remain on the ground.

For me, it was the most memorable performance I have ever given. I shall never forget the power of that inner being, and I have since never underestimated it.

How could I describe it except for the words it spoke? The terror, the peril, the struggle were beyond anything I'd ever experienced. In retrospect, it did not intend to harm or threaten me. It was my own logical process that ravaged me.

When does it appear? When does it whisper? When does it draw you away to its own feathery world? I wish I knew, but I do know I long desperately for it and drop everything when I hear it breathing: to give myself to it, to bathe deeply in its pleasures. I cannot call it up. It reveals itself in unrelated ways. There are very few clues to its random logic. It defines itself in its own way and in its own time. It intrudes at the least likely moments. Its imagery gouges deeply.

I dreamt one night a dream of perfection, a dream of the perfect performance. I had always believed that with perfection everything was answered, that there was nothing further, not even hope. Perfection was a scary achievement. I never found this notion too disturbing, because it was almost impossible to achieve. Perfection had so many factors to coordinate, and besides, I had never seen perfection. I came close, very close, but never the achievement. Perfection was more a revelation than an actual arrival.

But in this dream I saw what it was.

The dream was an operatic scene. It involved a single singer, a woman. She was not a flesh-and-blood woman, but the embodiment of the ideal woman for that role. The notes she sang were the exact fulfillment of everything belonging to that note. The pitch, the timbre, the placement, the breath, the sound was not humanly produced, but rather came from a flawless source. Her gestures too were exact and inevitable. She held a small rectangular box. A perfectly proportioned box that she placed on a shelf that surrounded the box as if they were essential to each other.

Her hair was blond and hung loosely but in clusters with a glittering thread in it. She wore a pale blue dress. She finished her aria and everything faded.

I had seen and heard perfection. I did not awaken but realized I had been awake all the while. I had witnessed perfection in a waking moment. Then I felt an extraordinary peace. I tried desperately to revisualize what I had seen. What had elevated it out of all reality? Surely everything I witnessed was real. I thought back to everything I could remember. The performance was so easy, so effortless. Perfection was its own thing. It was above the fact. It had an identity that existed concurrently with the doing. Everything in that scene bespoke itself. There were no imbalancing intrusions anywhere in her performance. Vividly etched, it was so easy, so calm, so undisturbed, yet so disturbing.

Perfection is not a goal, like a target to be struck by a performing arrow. Perfection is always there. It runs parallel to the doing. Occasionally you shift onto that concurrent track and for a moment you are coasting on perfection. Throughout a career, you ride those concurrent rails for longer and longer spans of time until, for those who are blessed, they merge, allowing artists to become translucent and reveal to the audience the internal mechanisms of their art.

It is all a matter of getting to the inside of movement, the inside of dance, the inside of self, always remembering that one's greatest treasures are usually worthless to others, and maintaining the faith.

For performing artists, immortality does not come when they are gone. They may reach it a hundred times before they leave the scene. They may sit with the gods and, on exalted occasions, converse with them.

Others think of immortality as an afterwards, as a legacy. The dancer knows it as now. I have known immortality many times. When I leave the stage and become mortal, I feel foolish, because mortals wait for mortality before they think of immortality. I die when I return to mortals and when I no longer can reach the living immortality of performance. Perhaps, when my turn comes, I will journey into the immortality of death, as a way of living.

Immortality is piercing.

Cruelty can rest in the muscles as well as in the mind.

65

There is always the terror that one will open a door and stand before some blinding, searing presence, a terror of being consumed. How different from the childhood terror of the dark. In that darkness, the unknown would pounce upon me. But with the blinding light, it would call my name and I would vanish. This is the dark side of light.

The dark hours . . .

When the end appears. Adjusting to the end of a career.

One night at 4 A.M., when my mind was at its most lucid, I woke with a realization that drove me from my warm bed to my desk. "What if," I thought, "during these periods of totality, these awesome moments when artists are in complete control of themselves and their art, they are not living an experience for the first time, but rather reliving it. Suppose from their enormous memory bank they have relived a reality. Have we lived everything once before? And is our current life merely selected relivings?

"These relivings are not surface scratching or recalls, or *déjà vu*s, but participations of magnitude for the brain and sentient systems. Is this what hallucinogens create—relivings? Is that what people who take drugs search for? Are they reaching for these illuminations as part of their lives as do artists and saints?

"For sociological reasons, we all must live together. But if man is a universe unto himself, then much of that universe has already been explored and stored, to be relived at another time and experienced fully during another life that may afford him more time to do so. Perhaps the moment of reliving is what we call the moment of 'now.'"

I wrote this much and then went back to bed. The next morning I read it and thought, better not think this through, it looks frightening. You're a sentient person, don't provoke your brain. You've seen madmen, you know how easily the mind can turn on you.

I am convinced that these periods of totality, these awesome moments when artists are in complete control of their art, are moments of reliving an experience from their enormous memory bank. These moments are so blinding that laypeople, should they have them, are seriously disturbed because they have not been prepared for them as artists are. Artists begin with momentary experiences of this magnitude and try to expand them for longer periods. Eventually they bring this awareness into their living ethic.

When one experiences a cellular reliving, it is a total body experience, not simply a recall or a vague remembrance. Those untrained in physical and sentient training, as a dancer is, may see it as a spiritual awakening or calling. Dance artists make nothing special of these revelations other than to know that this is the standard for aesthetic achievement in performance. If they arrive at less, they are cheating or shortchanging their art; if they go beyond, they will reach greatness and genius.

Journal (1957). David Berlin

On Death

THE FIRST TIME DEATH appeared to me was with Jimmy
Waring's passing. I'd known Jimmy since I was twenty years
old. We became very fast friends during our early years. Both
of us had an inkling of our destinations, though perhaps not of
our destinies, and this vision bound us closely. We both had visions
and high hopes, and the open door before us drew us even closer. In
a great many ways we held little in common. His direction in dance
was through the disciplines of ballet, mine were totally unformed.
He had a great concern for detail and placement, I simply lusted to
move. But we took each other very seriously, while our elders found
us both curious. He was my age and he died. Should I be thinking of
death?

In Taiwan, on a gray day with rolling clouds heralding the
desperately awaited monsoon, a short note in the *China Press*, the
American newspaper, announced "Gower Champion dies at 59"
on the eve of his latest production. This time death came forcefully.
I was struck. The blow came to my stomach and my heart. I
lowered the paper, half expecting tears. And they came, internally.
I remembered thinking, how curious to cry inside your face.

The first time I'd met Gower was backstage; he attended a
performance. Nik sent someone upstairs for me, to my dressing
room at the Henry Street Playhouse, "There was someone who
wanted to meet me, would I come down?" I spotted Gower
immediately. He looked radiant. Healthy, tanned, exuding the

animal life of a man in great physical condition. We talked and I was overwhelmed by his compliments.

He was on top of the world then, and I had to teach a children's class the next morning at 9 A.M. I couldn't fathom two more opposite worlds. He had brought some other Hollywood stars with him and they drifted back to Nik, but he lingered with me and continued to talk. When I returned to my dressing room, I realized how terrible I looked. Makeup half on, half smeared off. A torn rehearsal sweatshirt covering me. Not at all the Hollywood picture of a star receiving guests in his dressing room. It hasn't changed much over the years. Later that night at dinner, I realized Gower's looks and conversation were admiring of my unaffected mien, and that was the way it should have been.

When Nik received his *Dance Magazine* Award, I suggested that Gower make the presentation. Nik was reluctant for a moment, then welcomed the idea. Gower said on presentation, "I'm the flip side of the Nikolais record."

And then there was the exhilaration of *Hello, Dolly!* Pure joy, a delicious froth consumed in one mouthful and then gone.

Before I left on this most recent tour, I was going to ask Gower if I could sit in occasionally during a rehearsal of his new musical *42nd Street,* but realized I would be on tour then. Now halfway across the earth, in China, I read he had died.

I find the inner man lives more vividly now as the outer man becomes more garish. That participation with life becomes more embarrassing, more contrived daily as the soul thrives.

I grow more reluctant daily to meet and be with people, because they expect you to talk to them. I know I have been wrapped in the early web of death. The first stages of making my peace with the world.

When I arrived in Hong Kong, it was a very gray day. Everything was gray, and I suddenly thought: death is not black, death is gray.

Death first came to me as a thought and then as a presence. As a thought it wore a gauzy film, fluttering and opening to appear and disappear. As a presence, it cast a chalky calm, and then I saw the face. It was not at all frightening. It was composed and so bored. I think death has lost interest.

Chimera (1966). Bob Greene

The Inner Person

THE PHYSICAL BODY COMES of age with the ceremony of puberty. The arrival of semen and blood are heralded with admittance into the tribe. The prizes of man and womanhood are handed out in the form of physical change. It appears that nature's first concern is the renewal of the species.

But similarly and subtly, without the noisy trumpets of orgasm, there is also the coming of age of the soul. The puberty of the inner man.

It was a dry, hot summer day. Alone on a tree-lined, sleepy street in Brooklyn, I sat on a small bench before the low two-family house. Friends, the few I had, had all gone somewhere for the day. Where? Perhaps the beach, but gone nevertheless.

Why was I alone? I wondered. I was not really alone. On the other end of the bench a little girl played busily and absorbedly with her doll. But I was alone and restless. Worse, I knew I was alone and I felt the restlessness.

I moved to the stone steps before the house preparing to enter, but stopped and sat down on a step.

Why was I here? Why was I alone? There was no reason for me to be there.

The child continued to play and talk to her doll. She scolded the doll for wrinkling its dress and then proceeded to fix the offender's clothing.

Why was I watching this? I walked to the patch of garden. I

stared at the two flowers and the woody hedge. I sighed a huge sigh and returned to the bench.

Suddenly the little girl's play voice penetrated my mind.

She baby-talked to her doll. Her make-believe was very real. On and on she went, totally absorbed, totally believing.

How could she not realize she was not alone? How could she not realize how bored I was? Why was she behaving like a child?

And in that moment I realized she was a child, and it was I who was no longer a child. I had grown up. I could recognize childishness. As I later realized, my inner man had made itself known, my soul had come of age.

In the same way, one can discover eternity in a moment. Like its outer physical counterpart, the soul has its birth, its puberty, and its maturation. Some develop early, some develop late. Some never develop.

There is the body, the mind, the emotions, and the soul, each one a distinct entity.

Medical science traces and defines the physical body and its intricacies. The emotions are the rewards for staying alive. The emotions have no responsibility and pass freely, pleasuring the appetites, lending passion and flavor to the heart, the stomach, and the genitals.

Psychology evolved as a science to deal with the mind and its as yet undiscovered ramifications. But the soul was left to the mysteries of the church, and religion to esoteric philosophers who shunted it to the realm of the hereafter to be dealt with in the next world. But the truth is, the soul is a very active part of the daily life experience. It influences all judgments. It controls the emotions and brings a special value to all experiences. It tempers bestiality, spices sloth, and flavors reason. The participation of the soul comes naturally, because it is there. Above all, it allows us our greatest judgmental tool, intuition. In a career of wide intuitive awareness, I've found the intuition seems to exist outside of the body, adhering to us like a second skin, prickling our bodies with uneasiness and forewarning. Perhaps the intuition breathes and feeds on our pores, and sends its messages to us through them.

This inner person houses our conscience, our sense of honor, morality, truth, belief, and justice, among other things, factors that science, as a science, is very uncomfortable with. There are also darker sides to its nature, as there are dark sides to the emotions and the mind. The soul is faceless and without physical identity. Would we, if the occasion ever occurred, recognize our own soul, if we came face to face with it?

This inner person is the closest friend we have, the one we trust most. We talk to it all the time. Constantly we ask its advice, and constantly we allow outer forces with their diversions and distractions to tempt us from that advice.

I think, in this day and age, we can call that inner being the soul, and as such not confuse it with the mind. There are few who have not dealt with themselves as double beings: the inner and outer self. The intrinsic problem was that the mind and the soul were considered as one, whereas the brain was the link between the soul and the mind, the physical joining and coordinating of the two like a Siamese twin.

That the body, mind, emotions, and soul are all inextricably bound, housed as they are within the same organism, is a fact. Whether they are always in accord is another matter.

Performers have dealt with these varied operations and divergencies many times and have forced themselves to recognize and deal with their individuality. They have trained themselves to move fluidly from one to the other and orchestrate them in various combinations as well.

The inner person does not live on a diet of protein and fat. It is always awake, not like the mind, housed as it is in the conscious and subconscious that need periods of rest, and not like the emotions that babble and pick with their cavalier and random appetites.

The soul had a better time of things during the ages of superstition, in the early and ancient days. It knew how to deal with the unknown. It made the decisions while the brain was being developed. In recent times, the brain and its capabilities have developed so rapidly that recent human evolution is made plainly evident by the developments of and within the brain.

The inner person is what makes artists unique. It dictates the quality of their work, and how they handle the materials of their art. When they are at one with their art, the intuitive judgment guides their hand. Selecting, structuring, texturing, and all their sensibilities from touch to transcendency have major input from the inner person.

Artists must have a god of some sort. They must have a supreme deity whom they can rail against, accuse, and denounce for all the injustice in the world, which means for all the injustice the world has shown the artists and their work. They also need a god to whom they can cuddle up when they lick their wounds, and to whom the more unselfish can give thanks for their good fortune and blessings.

All artists are religious. Their art is evidence of their belief. Do they worship a deity? Who knows? But they do worship what the deity stands for.

When artists talk to their muse, it is not the buxom Greek draped lady they converse with, but rather the voice from within, the work upon which they are laboring. They listen to it to tell them how the work should develop. The muse disguises itself within the work in progress. Sometimes it shapes itself as sound, or color, or movement. Sometimes it'll sit in the eye and judge. Sometimes it'll be the work. Sometimes it won't appear for days, and at other times, its presence is relentless and carping.

The muse can be consoling and sing sweet songs of success, and suddenly she will turn her back and startle you with her obscenities.

Yet, throughout her periods of intimacy, she is never intimate. Her guard is never down. She will only be worshiped, never addressed. She plays no favorites, and her standards are never the same from work to work, from performance to performance.

The eyes of the imagination cannot stand the strong light. Their lids lift with the first darkness and at night open wide. The trees grow taller when seen from below. The dark coolness bathes the skin differently, and fear opens the way to the necessary unknown.

People think it is the moon that drives men mad. But they are mistaken. It is the sun that breaks the mind. Moon madness makes one see all too clearly, a lucid vision "sans merci." The sun melts the mind, fusing the thoughts into slag, rough-edged, raw, turning wine to acid, and glory to tears.

The eyes are responsible for so much. What they see will be remembered, what they tell us we will know. The soul wearies sometimes because the eye has seen too much.

The inner person is informed and nourished by the sensory process of the body. It is imperative that the care and feeding of it must be high on the priority list of maintenance.

The life and the working process of an artist are inextricably bound together, but not always compatible. The extremes of the soul are indeed difficult to relate to each other. The dark side lets in very little light, and the sun can be blinding. One is sealed, the other exposed. The night has dark things to imply, and the sun is blatant and cannot hold a secret.

The inner and the outer being have different weaknesses and strengths, and different moral obligations. When the standards for one are applied to the other, there is often an incompatibility that results in a third factor called guilt.

The reasonings of the half-world are the memories that talk and shout, and never cease their whisperings.

Oh, what has been buried behind these doors, these walls, under the floors. The soul can be, and often is, a cesspool of memories. It was the dark side of the soul that Pandora released when she opened the box. Her second gift was hope. Hope, an essential nourishment for the inner person: the food a dancer lives on.

Touring *Junk Dances* (c. 1968)

The Grand Manner

ARTISTS, UNTIL THE 19TH century, were always at the mercy of some sort of patronage, either by the church, royalty, or secular wealth.

By the 20th century, the theater had become a substantially independent business venture. With the rise of audience numbers from the middle class, the number of theaters increased rapidly, as did the roster of performers.

One of the ambitions of the middle class was to sample the social life of the aristocracy. High among these temptations were the theater, the opera, and the ballet. Social reform and democracy changed many things. With the decline of aristocratic privilege went the practice of the Grand Manner.

The Grand Manner, in the courtly sense, always implied extravagance: a cavalier reward of an emerald necklace to a favorite ballerina, a carriage and fine horses in tribute to the divinity of a diva, a ring drawn from a royal hand and pressed into the sweaty palm of a panicked virtuoso.

Impulsive, acts of calculated carelessness, generous, often sincere, these were the outbursts of the Grand Manner. Lavish after-theater dinners, profusions of flowers, excessive candlelight, and all of it reflected endlessly in the laboriously hand-polished chandeliers.

The style of the Grand Manner was always big, lavish, excessive, and extreme. In the Grand Manner, one was never concerned with wealth or value, only with the impression it made. The Grand Manner was a club that not many could literally afford, and in a way, it was a championship with a floating trophy. The winner came from the ranks of the prestigious, who were often motivated in turn by excessive drink, impressive erudition, or a feeling of guilt that compelled them to patronize the arts.

In the old days, if a lord had nothing else to give, he gave a village.

But these were the memorable monuments that stood alongside the road of patronage. The pavement itself, however, was constituted of thousands of lesser-sung generosities. Fundings that paid the rent and bought the bread and helped produce the art.

The Grand Manner depended upon enormous incomes and limited ambition while the new middle class operated the other way around. Their enormous ambitions could not quite match their limited resources. The Grand Manner was mostly a matter of money that the middle class simply could not afford and, when they could, they felt guilty about spending it and consequently handled largess awkwardly.

The opera houses, before the various revolutions, were under the patronage of their royal highnesses. When the States became sponsor, they could no longer handle the responsibility for the Grand Manner and let it fall pretty much into the hands of the performing artists.

Under the royal patronage, the artists were in no position to practice their temperament because the consequences could be severe. But with the commercial sponsors, performers could now whet and hone their temperaments to outrageous degrees, which sometimes created legendary tales. Eventually the trappings and manner of a by-now defunct aristocracy were absorbed with relish by the royalty of the theater. After all, they now possessed the clothing, the jewels, and the necessary overbearing egos. They now swayed the multitudes. Bernhardt, Barrymore, Caruso, Callas, Duncan, Pavlova, and others soon set a standard for a theatrical aristocracy.

What characterized the Grand Manner now was the demand for quality displayed in the most extravagant way, whatever the cost. This was a perfect maxim for the great performers because, even if sometimes they were a little lacking in discerning quality, they certainly knew extravagance.

Extravagance comes at a price and price means payment. Certainly most artists cannot afford these prices, but some know how to go about getting things paid for. They practice hauteur, bearing, condescension, seduction, glamour, style, aloofness, and rage, all of which gets someone to provide the necessary funds.

Expensive quality, be it represented by exquisite costumes or buckets of French champagne, costly suppers at which the artists can arrive fashionably late dressed elegantly and hold court, dressing rooms filled with flowers and exotic plants, all provide the proper environment in which the Grand Manner can thrive and bloom.

And then there is the manner itself. By now the Grand Manner had defined itself as a performing style. A chilling look, a dismissing gesture of the hand, a turn of the head, a flick of a cigarette, all so effective on stage, and so devastating off. Some artists call the manner a game. Some feel it to be a necessary duty. But all know its importance in "keeping the distance."

Many years ago, a host of a popular television program that usually featured stars from the performing arts as well as popular artists had as his guest Lily Pons, the great diva. The host himself came from the pop world of Broadway show business and sports. His habit was very hail-fellow-well-met. Lots of slaps on the back and democratic chumminess.

On this one occasion, after Mlle. Pons had finished "The Bell Song," he walked towards her, lifting his arm to embrace her in his usual show-biz way. She turned towards him and drew her barely-five-foot height up to a towering seventy-five feet and looked down at him. His hand froze in midair. Lakme, the Daughter of the Regiment, Thais, Delilah looked at him, and her eyes said, "Keep your distance." The television camera caught all of this, and the effect was very telling. The aristocracy of the arts are not that available.

Maintaining the Grand Manner in the United States is very difficult today. The equality that we strive for in a democracy has proved more leveling than uplifting, and the distance of time back to those aristocratic days has made those "old days" all but a memory that grows dimmer with every year. The very idea of the Grand Manner is fast disappearing. One might almost ask, "Is it natural for cream to rise to the top, or has homogeneity become indigenous to the udder?"

Today castles are museums through which everyone may wander. They become available to anyone for a shilling. Dressing opulently for the theater has in recent times become unsafe. There is a limit on generous tax-deductible gifts, and the press has a field day with the exceptional spender.

One of the weaker attempts at maintaining the Grand Manner is playing the jet set and acquiring status symbols, which are the dregs of prestige. The big difference here is the originals led the way, whereas jet-setters always seem to be following someone.

There was one man, however, who represented a last flame of aristocratic Grand Manner in America. Sol Hurok, born in autocratic Russia, Jewish and impoverished but extravagant of soul, surrounded his artists with style and shamelessly spoiled them, which made for legendary artists and legendary performances. Although his name was always prominent on the billboards and he had by this time developed the charisma of the grand impresario, nevertheless, when he was with great artists, he always remained in the background. He never shadowed their luster. He knew how to seduce the best from his artists. He knew the power of the Grand Manner and of quality, and he always made it pay off, especially at the box office.

The Grand Manner is indeed a thing of the past. So are carriages and velvet. Incessant press coverage tends to perforate personalities before they can become legends. There is a cruel and unhealthy tendency in America to tear down rather than elevate its heroes. The robes of the past are encrusted with glory, although some of the linings have been dragged through the slime. The gems and brilliants of the Grand Manner have lent glamour to the dazzle of achievement and exposed some of its darker aspects.

With the Grand Manner, there usually comes a pecking order. From pettiness to snobbishness to exalted arrogance.

I had a friend, who has since died, who was born and raised in White Russia. The Russia of the Czars was the direct descendant of the Caesars of imperial Rome. Their privileges were mind-boggling, and their customs opulently Byzantine. She told me that when she was a girl her mother would sometimes travel to Paris. On these trips she would take along every household item, linen, silver, and bedding, because the West was so barbaric, they never knew what they could expect. When I got to know Ella she was impoverished, living with her spoiled and slightly insane forty-five-year-old son in a small, beautifully decayed villa in the south of France.

She was then about eighty. Her bearing was the sort that would not take "no" for an answer. Nikolais and I visited her one day and invited her to lunch at a local restaurant. From the moment she entered the dining room, everyone deferred to her, including the maître d'. She marched without any hesitancy into the kitchen and inspected the food, lifting all the pot lids and poking at all the food. She made a selection for all of us, and then joined us at the table. "This is not a very good restaurant," she said in the loud voice of the elderly, "but it's all we have."

The waiters, the cook, the owners all waited for her approval of everything served, and I must say it was an exceptional meal, although I had by this time shrunk so low into my seat with embarrassment, I could hardly reach the table.

The Grand Manner has always belonged to the wealthy, not only with money but rich in eccentricity. One thing I do know about those with the Grand Manner is that, if they cannot succeed in intimidating someone else to pay the bill and must pay it themselves, they most certainly never count the change.

Entre-Acte (1959). Sosenko

Benefactors

WHEN ONE LOOKS AT a painting, be it Bosch or Bruegel, Rousseau or de Chirico, the eye cannot be hasty. For either symbolically or humanly, hidden or suggested, there are other people or forces tucked in the corners, hovering behind exotic foliage or casting long shadows, who are integral to the canvas as a whole.

The profession of dance is like such a canvas. Although it is a performing art and its cast of characters is always evident and larger than life, there is more here than meets the eye. There are people and events who have helped both push and catapult the art forward. Some of these people are the benefactors.

Benefactors come from all circumstances. Some wish to remain anonymous, some contribute to see their name in lights. Some close the relationship with their signature at the bottom of a check. Others send along a bit of their heart. Some are duty bound to support the arts, others are heartbroken because they cannot do more. But they have always been individual people making individual commitments for individual satisfaction.

Benefactors are seen and their presence felt in many ways. Madame von Meck supposedly never met Tchaikovsky, whereas the Medicis' bossiness overwhelmed their artists. Theo sent more than a brotherly stipend to Vincent for his bizarre output.

The economics of dance do not bear a rosy hue, unless you like red ink. The profession is never relieved of financial pressure.

Dancers as a rule don't concern themselves with the financial dealings of a dance company. Their concerns are only aroused when their own contracts are involved.

Today, as superstars demand super salaries, and super fees demand super ticket prices, and super prices demand super audience attendance, and super audiences demand superhype, we can expect a super descent when all the hot air is expended from the balloon. What goes up, comes down, or burns up.

Although the dance product is marketed and saleable, what makes it costly is that it must be reproduced at every performance with all the cost that goes into initial production. It cannot be stockpiled. It is perishable beyond belief, and it exists on the frailty of human nature.

With these absurd business recommendations to its credit, it is easy to understand why dance cannot go it alone in the marketplace. The arts have always lived in thin soil; it is their condition. They must grow in thin soil in order to survive in thin soil.

Fortunately there are people who respond to the endless pleas for funds to support this risky profession. Funding the arts is as essential as nursing a baby. Neither could possibly survive without assistance and care. Both are essential to the existence of a society. As dancers are implanted with a need to move, so are benefactors instilled with the need to give. They too have been chosen. They have been given the responsibility to care.

Generosity often is not generous to the donor. It sometimes bears more bad will than good. If one is on the receiving end of largess, then all is well, if one is not then "fair is foul."

Three notable women, Lucia Chase, Eugenia (Delarova) Doll, and Rebekah Harkness, did much to help the dance. Each had artistic and performing ambitions that drew them to the dance. They came from different convictions, and shaped their lives from those dictates. One came from a New England ethos, another from European civility, and the third was an outspoken midwesterner. Personally they had little in common. Their upbringing and sensibilities had different controls. They lived partly happily and fulfilled, partly in chaos. There is no profession in art more volatile than dance. There is no constancy in dance because it is based on the most inconsistent instrument, the human body, and its erratic temperament.

LUCIA CHASE (1907–1986)

Lucia Chase, until 1980, was the American Ballet Theatre. She helped give birth to it, formed it, nursed it through its adolescence, directed its education and bought it its first pair of long pants, rocked it while it cut its teeth, washed its diapers, and buffered it from reviews worse than death. She shaped, pushed, and bullied it to allow it to find its identity, and became, and rightly so, fiercely possessive of it.

But more than all this, she succeeded—even more than that—she triumphed.

Of course she didn't do this alone. She worked with Richard Pleasant and Oliver Smith, judicious advisors in all matters scenic, choreographic, musical, and financial, whose advice she filtered through her own canny intuition to produce a potent result.

The first time I met Lucia Chase was at an ABT performance at the Metropolitan Opera House in Lincoln Center. We had both arrived late and were held at the door by a young usher. He apologized, but we could not enter. The curtain had just gone up. I was speechless that he could keep Miss Chase out of the auditorium until I realized he probably did not know her.

"Look," I said, "this lady is Lucia Chase. She rented this theater and that's her company on stage. You are at this moment in her employ."

Poor boy, he was abject. He did not recognize her, and by now there were six others at the door. He had no choice. "I'm sorry," he said, "but you'll have to view the first act in the television room." He directed us to it and we all went off.

Throughout all of this Miss Chase said nothing. I took her arm. "Why didn't you tell him who you are?" I asked.

"It's all right," she assured me.

We went to the late room and watched the thirty-two girls make their entrance in *La Bayadère*. Not many people in her position would have found that situation "all right."

The creative record and performing roster of ABT is its own clear proof of its greatness. The quantity and quality of its output far exceed any producer of ballet as a theatrical form, including Diaghilev. This is intended in no way to lessen Diaghilev's extraordinary achievements, but to make sure that our overfamiliarity with the recent does not diminish its value, especially when compared to legends.

Legends begin with infallibility and reverence. They have been cleansed and polished to erase all traces of foibles, cantankerousness, dubious taste, and flops.

Managing and directing a large ballet company is an awesome task. Hand-in-hand with all the glamour of opening nights and premieres rest the day-to-day problems of existence. Whose job is it to consider all those livelihoods, all those careers that constitute a dance company? Box-office receipts just about pay the rent today. The money to run a company must come from someplace, from someone, somehow. But more important than raising money is who worries about it, who understands that it must be done, and who does it, or sees that it is done.

Who, then, after this heavy burden, must face the daily intricacies of personality and personnel? How does one handle four great ballerinas all wanting to dance the same major classic role, other than presenting a season of only one three-act ballet, and giving everyone her turn in the leading role? "Why," screamed the press, "is Lucia Chase tormenting us with this season?" Some ridiculed her, some reviled, and, like children, once the mob spirit started, the blood ran high and they had a field day with their abuse.

But like the thoughtless children they were, I don't think any of them envisioned the painful scenes Lucia Chase had with those dancers who felt they had to dance those roles now before it was too late, who tearfully confessed their need to perform those roles for the challenge they presented, for the sense of achievement, for the completion it would bring to them as artists.

And would anyone else have yielded to these touching plaints, knowing the havoc it would create at the box office? It took a woman of stature, heart, guts, and a dash of worldly insanity, a woman like Lucia Chase.

"I've always done the dancers' contracts because I know them and they could talk to me. I understand them and they understand me. Now everything is so big. It's enormous. The thing is now so colossal that I can't even understand it. They talk in millions. They are trying to raise eight million this year. In the '50s it was $250,000. One needs an extraordinary staff for fundraising.

"There are no standing funds. We've used them up on emergencies. This profession is made up of half-engagements and half-emergencies.

"But the dancers are wonderful and the company is wonderful. You have to keep your dancers happy, and dancers want to perform. They're not happy if they don't.

"A sense of humor is very important. My father had a great sense of humor. I was brought up with the discipline to take care of myself. I tell all the dancers, discipline is just the greatest thing you can have. Being able to set your goal, stick to it, learn the skill to do it, and make good, honest decisions of things. It will help you face things and cope with things. I think ballet training is marvelous. It takes great discipline to train for ballet.

"For the first five years I was a completely happy dancer on stage, no thought of directing a company. I had so many wonderful years there, with Dick Pleasant and Oliver [Smith] and [Mikhail] Mordkin and Gene Loring, Anthony [Tudor], Agnes [de Mille], Jerry [Robbins], Lenny [Bernstein].

"Oliver and I continued to direct the company for thirty-five years. Ballet Theatre couldn't possibly have been without Oliver, he was marvelous."

What gave Lucia Chase her rounded abilities as a director? Was it her business acumen, her own acclaimed dancing career, her sagacity? And it was sagacity, regardless of what one thought went on under those fluffy locks, to be able to deal with the art and arithmetic that kept Ballet Theatre afloat and adventuresome all those years. It was more than anything her unflagging faith in the company. In all her years there, the organization faltered only once because of lack of funds.

Her belief and conviction in all the artists associated with Ballet Theatre filled the sails of that mighty vessel as it took off. She contributed regularly to the coffers, but her personal sense of honor always made her uncomfortable as she tried to balance her own dancing achievements, the managerial role thrust upon her, and her personal funds.

She gave the company stability. Somehow if Lucia was there, Ballet Theatre would always be there. If anyone pointed a finger at Ballet Theatre, they pointed it at her.

EUGENIA (DELAROVA) DOLL (1911–1990)

Eugenia Doll was a lady with an enormous enthusiasm for life, a long career as a dancer, and a very thick Russian accent. She also brought to the dance scene a set of values and judgments that are rare today because they reflected years of dance experience. During her marriage to Léonide Massine, she was very much a part of the Ballet Russe de Monte Carlo. She spoke vividly of how the dance today differed from her earlier participation in it.

I asked her what brought her to dance. What made her so committed?

"For me," she said, "it was theater in general. I loved the drama and acting, the dance and opera. It was the whole theater. I don't remember how I started because nobody in my family was ever on stage. I started in Russia, and when I got to Paris, I married Massine and we had a very glamorous life. To be an artist it was very important to be glamorous and beautiful. This was in the '30s before the war. There was still royalty, and the palaces and the best chateaus all over the world were often open to us.

"We were very popular and we were very social because we didn't work so hard. We had time to get dressed up and made up and go out. Now it's all such very, very hard work. We never said, 'We go to work.' We said, 'We go to dance.' Every rehearsal was to dance and now it is to work.

"We didn't do those crazy steps you do now. So many and so fast. We just stood quiet sometimes. All of this technique now is impossible and unbelievable. Every single dancer is suffering injuries. Dancing has become very painful work. We also worked hard, but it was more pleasure. We wouldn't have any injuries.

"You see, in Russia, in old days, [the] ballerina danced once a month. And on the day she danced, she never walked. And when she never walked, she held her head and feet up and she was carried in a carriage, and she never rehearsed that day. Oh, you can't imagine what it was like. Oh, we traveled a lot and we performed a lot and we did one-night stands, but the dancing wasn't so difficult.

"We jumped, naturally, beautifully and very high. The ones who couldn't jump high didn't. It is this terrific effort I am against. Even the greatest ballerinas must put in this effort. In modern dance too.

90

Same thing with ice skating. No more Sonja Henie with one beautiful turn in the air. Now three, four, up in the air.

"Somehow, then, there wasn't that speed, that stress. Before it was pleasure because you danced with pleasure. Now they have pleasure too, but you don't see it so much because they torture themselves. Too fast and too much, and sometimes it's contortions and sometimes a circus.

"We had trouble with some girls to lose weight. But we didn't have one single dancer that didn't have little bit difference from men. Now there is no difference. Only men have difference. The girls used to have a little bosom and they had little waist and they had little behind. You know, Diaghilev didn't like to have girls in tights. He said you didn't know when they were going to have a little too much someplace."

I asked her about Diaghilev.

"He traveled and he saw everybody. Everybody knew him and he knew everybody. When there was anything new, he could distinguish it. He found Stravinsky, he found Picasso, and in Moscow, from just talking to Massine, he could hear the talent. That's what we are missing now. There is nobody to bring these people together. Everyone is separated. Everyone works by themselves. They say there aren't any new composers, there aren't any artists, there isn't any this or that. It's impossible. There is. We must find them.

"When he came to rehearsals, he would watch and say, 'This is too long. This is wrong.' Now nobody does it. The longer the better. Still, ballet is wonderful."

The artistic director of most dance companies today is the choreographer. At an earlier time, this was not so frequently the case. The artistic director was a director of all the artistic efforts and did not see the creation of ballet from only one point of view. But now the responsibilities of the choreographers have become staggering. Most of them spend a great deal of their energies on noncreative matters. Very often these affairs are matters the choreographer has little skill in dealing with and, as a result, does badly.

"Choreographers have to be born with the talent, but the artistic director has to lead them. You have to give them ideas. You have to develop ideas. You have to come to rehearsals and start things. You have to change things. The scenery has to be right. The steps and lighting have to be right. All that doesn't exist very much today.

Very seldom, if it does at all. Everybody's by themselves. I see how it works today. Nobody can say a word. Everyone is afraid to say anything, except maybe when it's too late.

"The same thing with the scenery. They find one man and stick with him over and over again. If it's good, if it's bad, it doesn't matter. Again and again because nobody looks for the new talents.

"And critics, also, sometimes they don't give a new choreographer a chance. They right away pan. 'That's no good.' That's all. So the new choreographers go to Europe to create, because critics there are better. Not so important. Here it is very important. Diaghilev never listened to critics because he knew that if an artist had talent, it would develop each time more and more. You have to take chances. They did things that people threw tomatoes at and screamed and yelled, 'Boooo.' So what? They tried everything.

"Diaghilev wanted always new. When they asked him to come to America, he wanted to bring all modern. He wanted to bring Picasso's things, but the people here said, 'No—you've got to bring old things first.' Always old things first."

I asked her what she would like to see as a general direction for the dance.

"I was thinking that, in the future, I would like to see the two companies in one. Like Balanchine's and the Ballet Theatre in one. Have all the Balanchine ballets and the big ballets together. We should have more comedy ballets and maybe make some new fantasy, a new *Giselle*. I mean something entirely new. Something never done before.

"Dancers should do more things. They should know politics. They should read more, educate themselves more. Lots of people say dancers are dumb. Not dumb, devoted. Their devotion is unbelievable. Dancing is a hard, tough job. Tough work. Actually it is very uninteresting aside from being on the stage. You work hard, you look for a place to eat afterwards, and it's twelve o'clock at night, and tomorrow you start all over again. You need terrific devotion. You really have to be crazy to dance."

REBEKAH HARKNESS (1915–1982)

If ever there was a tragic figure in the world of benefactors, it must be Rebekah Harkness, who like Cleopatra "loved not wisely, but too well." No need to discuss her private life. If one were versed in Wagner's private life, one would never listen to his music. Human nature and its motivations are too complex to steer through them with any logic. What is important are the results.

She suffered the fate of an autocrat in a democracy. She behaved royally, a dangerous thing to do in America. She also innocently challenged the ballet hierarchy, who did everything they could to demolish all she built and eventually destroyed her. She was indeed Wednesday's child.

Never was there a patron of the dance in America such as she. She was indulgent with her artists as well as with herself. She was handsome, big-boned, and had great flair. Often her misguided generosity reflected her own flamboyant nature.

Once the underbrush of her personal life is cleared away, one cannot but be impressed by her contribution to the dance. On the level of production, she pushed several important American companies forward towards their later prominence. She gave those companies, then struggling on every level, a taste of the good life. The glamour, gracious working environments, travel, salaries, and style, all of which gave a new polish and luster to the profession. Everyone involved with her grew and felt their worth because her largess said, "You deserve this and this is what you should expect."

The dance in America stopped shuffling from foot to foot and stood up a little straighter.

Her personal ambitions were to be somehow involved in the productions. Although she took class every day, she never seriously aspired to be a dancer. Instead she focused on her limited skill as a composer. She was not a great artist by any means, but her musical successes and failures were on a par with the many other composers who have written for the dance. When she began her own company, the Harkness Ballet, she drew heavily upon and decimated the personnel of the Joffrey company, which she had once lavishly sponsored. The new company featured a wonderful roster of dancers and an impressive repertory, and established itself here and abroad. But the antagonism it created in America made her reluctant to further present the company here. The personal abuse from the press began. The contention here was the manner in which she engaged the Joffrey dancers. She offered them financial circumstances that the Joffrey company couldn't possibly match. It should be remembered that those dancers who left Joffrey left on their own volition. They signed their own contracts with Harkness, she did not abduct them.

This is not a profession in which to cast the first stone. This profession is practically built of glass.

One dancer, Lisa Bradley, noticeably refused to leave Joffrey. She remained and her beauty and artistry helped Joffrey survive. As a postscript, when Joffrey saw no further use for her in his repertory, and because he eschewed the star system, which she had then become, he did not renew her contract. (Wherever you are, Lisa, should you read this, I send you my love.)

Rebekah Harkness's belief in dance was consuming. For her own company, foreign companies, and New York City, and the United States for that matter, she rebuilt the Colonial Theater into the first dance theater in New York City, a theater designed exclusively for the dance. (The State Theater at Lincoln Center was built to house opera, musical comedy, and dance, and still functions as a multipurpose theater.) The auditorium flowed graciously onto the stage. The upholstery was soft blue velvet and the chairs were made of a light Spanish spruce. They were comfortable and had good sight lines. The stage was sprung and perfectly balanced for weight. Backstage the dressing rooms, dancers' lounge, and warmup room considered every need a dancer might have. The beauty and dance exclusivity of the theater would have filled any dancer's heart with pride. The one flaw was a large mural that surrounded the proscenium arch. It depicted dancers curling and sweeping upward to a central figure, like angels ascending towards the Madonna at the apex on high. Unfortunately, the pigment for the skin tone of the otherwise beautifully rendered (and some thought pornographic) figures was of an unhealthy greenish hue, and the figure crowning the tableau was of the benefactress Harkness herself.

Well, the press had a field day. They tore her apart. They couldn't wait to outdo each other in reviling phrases in review after review. The personal attacks on her were slanderous. Sure, the mural was a mistake, but the theater was priceless.

Her vision for the dance needs of the theater was to include renovating a nearby hotel to house visiting dance companies, particularly foreign companies who were virtually left adrift in the city. In time she could no longer tolerate the personal abuse and tore the theater down. Imagine, a new theater, barely broken in, was demolished, all at enormous expense. Shortly afterward she became a victim to cancer, and soon after that she died.

It seems like a dream to remember that so beautiful a theater

94

once existed in New York, a dance theater that would have given so much pride to the dance in America. An elegant, comfortable, and theatrically equipped theater that would have ranked with any of the beauties of the 19th century, yet with every 20th-century convenience, torn down by the howlings of the press. The theater was built and torn down in five years. What a loss!

The history of patronage for the dance in America is a small one. I may be wrong, but I don't think anyone gave more of their personal fortune to the art than Rebekah Harkness. Nor was there anyone more maligned for doing so. Today, her presence in dance can still be seen and felt through the Harkness Foundations and their generous support of the dance. At least posthumously, her good will not be "interred with her bones," but lives after her.

Lecture-Demonstration (c. 1974). Cheryl Walsh

96

Bucks

THE MOST DIFFICULT, INVOLVED, and costliest part of performance is the actual presentation of a production. Performing is a complicated business. Without the performing outlet, there would be no profession. The curtain goes up only when the audience is assembled.

Dances can be walked through and marked in a rehearsal room. Sets and costumes can be imagined during rehearsals, but the hovering presence of performance does not settle until there is an audience for it to settle upon.

Performances for the most part are sporadic. A home season, a tour, and then a hiatus, that awful suspension of performing sensibilities. The performer tries desperately to bridge the performing highs, but every suspension bridge can only span a limited distance, and then it sags and lowers. Scheduling performances is very complicated, and often done years in advance. There is nothing more chilling to a dancer than to learn that in a year or two a major season is being planned. What does a year really mean to a dancer who is struggling to sustain a honed condition from day to day, and can only do so upon the whetstone that an audience provides? What would a surgeon do if he operated on such a sporadic schedule?

In Paris, during her years there, Isadora Duncan would never torment herself with enforced inactivity, but instead would send invitations to friends informing them that she would dance on whatever day she felt inclined. There, in her studio, before her blue curtains, she would dance for thirty or so guests. What a lesson there is to learn from this simplicity, what strength to draw from this solution.

If a dancer must perform, then perform. But, alas, ego doth make us prideful, and to dance before thirty people is too violent a fall from pride, especially when one considers how interwoven are pride and the erect placement of the backbone. Pride envisions devoted multitudes tearing at and expanding the pulsing heart, straining the lungs, forcing adulation and accolades upon a trembling god.

Thirty people? Too painful, too humiliating.

But Isadora did it. In her early career, Isadora did not worry about finances. She was gracious enough to let others do it for her. Her lover Singer, heir to the sewing machine fortune, allowed for this idyllic situation of dancing where and when she chose. Would that be the case for all of us. But, alas, performing is a costly business.

I discovered early that, without the independent means to do one's work, there would be no work. Waiting for others to provide means was unpredictable and consequently unproductive. Without a company for a choreographer to create upon, there is no choreography.

And so a major part of my efforts were spent in raising money, a task I hated. Maintaining a company was vital, and in time I faced the depressing realization of how much this unpleasant task was draining me. More than once I swore to chuck the whole humiliating process of raising funds. More than once an artistic success drew me back.

I thought regularly of how different things might have been if I had pursued a career as a soloist, if I had gone it alone. Of how many opportunities I forfeited to support a company. But the memory of that one solo concert would return to me, and I realized I had no choice but to take the route I did.

In the early 1960s, I was invited to do a solo concert in Los Angeles. It was a weekend of performances. I had suggested the solo format because I was curious to see if I could do it.

It was a great success. The public and press were overwhelming. It was more than I had hoped for. But a frightening thing happened backstage. I was alone. I had never been without the excitement of other dancers around me. There was no energy, no tension, only a

98

calm quiet. The room speaker did not pick up the audience noise, and I was left with nothing but my imagination to prepare me for the stage.

When the curtain rose and applause greeted my entrance, I was shocked by the sound, and all my sensibilities were at odds with each other. I struggled all evening to find my performing center. I could not bear the loneliness of backstage, and I never did another solo concert. I could not bear being alone with my own thoughts before I appeared.

For twenty years, Nik and I worked at the Henry Street Playhouse, which was part of the Henry Street Settlement House. The business arrangements were such that the Settlement paid for the maintenance and overhead of the building and a small portion of the salaries. Through performances and a successful school, we managed to sustain a company and staff.

When Nik arrived in 1948, his budget was $1,000. When we left in 1969, it was $60,000. During that time, there was no need for a separate board of directors, or any necessity to raise funds. However, when we left the Playhouse, we had a distinct handicap. We had no experience in forming boards or fundraising.

The success and performing income of both companies sustained us to the tune of 95 percent of our expenses. But by the mid-'70s we began to face serious deficits, and here at the beginning of the '90s, they are more serious than ever. The arts today are sophisticated business ventures, and any artist planning a career had better study profit and loss as well as *pliés* and *relevés*. The profession is so artificially structured that being an artist takes second place to being a businessperson.

In 1965, the National Endowment for the Arts had finally gotten off the ground, and Nancy Hanks had brought stability to this unheard-of miracle. This lovely and gracious woman had brought together the mentalities of both Congress and the American artist, a feat that should have brought her a place in the pantheon of the gods. In order to serve the dance community, it was necessary for the companies seeking assistance to be structured along the necessary government guidelines, which basically meant forming for themselves a "not-for-profit organization," which then could receive government grants as well as tax-deductible funds from the private sector.

Now everyone who hoped to receive funds had to become a legal "not-for-profit organization," and with that status came all the encumbrances that it implied: board of directors, business managers, legal representation, fundraisers, as well as all the printed material they required. This led to directors of development and benefit parties. All of this meant additional staff who barely raised their own cost. A dead end if ever there was one.

In addition, there was still the pressure of booking.

The original concerns of supporting dancers and choreography, finding and paying for rehearsal space, commissioning new music, costumes, and production costs were all left begging as the administrative expenses mounted. This supposed bonanza of funding had instead torn apart the frail fabric of the art. The greed in every management came to the fore as everyone fought, connived, politicked, and worse to get at the limited funds.

The mayhem did not occur until later, because in the earlier guidelines a program known as the Dance Touring Program kept a balance. It allowed free enterprise to exist. The DTP supported presenters with one-third support of the artists' fees. The audience appeal and professional value of the companies determined the number of bookings and hence the amount of support. It was an open market. The companies did not receive the money. It came to them from the sponsors, who were now able to afford their fees and to take the risk of engaging dance events on an otherwise musically oriented season. The sponsors were still responsible to their audiences and to their own financial accountability. It was not in their nature to take risks.

Until the '60s, the concert bookings across the country were of a musical nature. Audiences were familiar with musical artists and ensembles. Soloists and orchestras could appear with little additional expense to the sponsor. A piano, chairs, and music stands were usually the extent of production costs. Now dance companies were asking for floors, lights, technicians, and sound systems. They were making costly demands, and as yet hadn't proven themselves either at the box office or in terms of their dependability. Contracts were being signed a year in advance, and many dance companies would disappear or would not be able to honor their agreements.

But some presenters took chances and broke the ice. Once these respected people took the plunge, then many others followed suit. Once they gave their approval to the new dance, many other sponsors opened their lists and a new wave of American modern dance poured across the country.

Concurrent with this and the NEA Dance Touring Program was the fortuitous fine arts and theater-building programs on the campuses. Campuses as a rule have long-range building programs, planned well in advance, and for various reasons give certain departments priority, depending on where the money and prestige rests. It could be the physical education departments with prominent sports teams, or the science departments with lucrative government contracts, and down the list. By some incredible coincidence, it was time, across the country, for the performing arts to have their day. And what a glorious day it was. The most important campus theaters were strewn like architectural gems across the country.

With new and fine facilities, a subsidy from the NEA to cover box-office losses, booking managers opening their rosters, and strong dance companies with new programs, the dance in America took off.

The honeymoon did not last more than five years, because in the later '60s the student revolution on the campuses brought student intercession into the choice of programs to be brought to the campus, and this meant chaos. Which student representatives were to be on the deciding committees was often not decided until the last minute, and then changed regularly. With such constant change on the committees and the need to book a year in advance, the touring seasons became impossible to plan as they had been before. Often companies would arrive to new hosts who had nothing to do with their being booked and on occasion were hostile towards them.

The older sponsors began to retire, and soon touring became a business. The courtesies with which they had once charmed their artists fell rapidly to the callousness of business as usual. There was a new order in the air. The scented times began to sour. The flower child became a memory pressed between the pages of Vietnam and narcotics.

I learned, too, that good contracts were made in good restaurants, the way good marriages are made in heaven, and then unfortunately the details were left in the hands of the people who never knew heaven. And soon faults, oversights, mismanagement, confusions,

101

buck-passing all occurred. The horrors of oversight played themselves out. And all the while, the need to meet the budget that dictated the lives of thirty people would stare pleadingly at me.

When the union struck our organizations, it shook Nik. All the sacrifices he had made for his company, all the long relationships he had made with his company members were slammed shut. He could no longer deal directly with his company, but had to go through the union and have a union representative present if he talked to them as a group.

But what threw a barb into his skin that still remains there today, and I don't think can ever be removed, was when his company brought him up for charges, and then magnanimously asked that the charges be dropped. From that day on, he lost all interest in his company. They had become a work force and he was management.

I joined AGMA, the dancer's union, in the early '50s, and remain a dues-paying member today. I never had any faith in its effectiveness because the profession was so poor, and dancers danced when they could and because they "had" to. I remain a member because I feel there should be some semblance of representation should the time ever come when it might be able to help the profession.

Unions, for all their virtues, were instrumental in bringing about the change from pleasure to work. By contracting on a tradesman basis, they brought about an automatic forty-hour work contract. Artists don't work forty hours a week, they work one hundred hours and more. But now they cannot. They are breaking the union rules if they do so, and all those involved can be severely penalized.

The artists worked hard and fought for this contract. It protected them from a great many injustices, but it did make a job of their profession. Choreography and the creation of new ballets suffered most with these time limitations because it also made a forty-hour creative week.

There is a sharp distinction between the time necessary to rehearse an already choreographed repertory and the time to create that repertory. Choreographers need time to erase, throw out, and redo their choreography. When over time pressure began to squeeze the creative pipeline, there was little chance for the necessary refinement to take place. Choreography is neither produced on a production line nor stockpiled in advance. It happens in a room with dancers and right then and there. As an art that is a fact. No union can change that. Force or threaten as they will, the fine print for creativity does not include any restrictions, least of all of time.

As dance organizations grew, the sickness of building on deficits grew with it. Earned income, once the sole source of survival, could no longer pay the mounting expenses. Unearned income now became not the occasional bonanza, a time for rejoicing, but a desperate need.

Unearned income no longer depended on the quality of choreography and dancing as did earned income, but was a wily world unto itself, with other standards and other mentalities. It was a world where manipulation, seduction, and statistical style counted. Soon the hunt was on for manipulators, seducers, and grant writers. The greatest difficulty was the paucity of dance administrators who had the skill to obtain unearned income and prepare the necessary applications.

Throughout the US, primarily on campus, arts administration programs were created and, in a sense, an assembly line of personnel was produced to help fill this need. The government took to offering its grants on a matching basis so that companies would not grow dependent on federal and state funds. This made it essential for companies to concentrate on private monies and effective, fundraising boards of directors.

It became clear that those companies with effective fundraising abilities were going to rise to the top, and those with weaker thrust were going to sink. Public hype and image became an effective force in bringing "names" to the attention of foundations and other private sources. This meant adding more staff to an already unbalanced situation and, quite frankly, dollars and cents have today taken prominence over creative and aesthetic output.

When the Dance Touring Program was abandoned, the one strong means that every company had to present their work on the open market was taken from them. Sponsors panicked and withdrew, sources of performing income dried up, and only those companies with strong PR outlets and strong fundraising personnel could continue their work.

Today it is a fundraising game; they hold all the cards. Boards of directors are looked upon as the real stability of a dance company. The field has become a merry-go-round of transient staffs and, in the midst of all this, the artistic directors have lost control of the art.

It has been tugged from them by the slick professionalism of the fundraising game.

Stability, which is that ability to plan the necessary year in advance, has more than ever found itself trying to keep its balance on shifting sands. With the passing of the strong, central figures, the magnetic poles about which so much dedication was focused will have to be rediscovered to maintain the individual character of dance companies in order for them to survive.

The heart, talent, and belief of the original company name-bearer can never be substituted, that we know, but the next directors are part of the new game. The artistic director constantly asks, "Where are we going? Is it to make new works or to stay alive, and can you have one without the other? Can I worry about all this alone? Can anyone handle this alone?"

Existence today is a shared job. Executive directors, boards, benefactors, and artistic directors are now bonded together by the glue that raising funds necessitates.

Entre-Acte (1959). Sosenko

Speed

SPEED IS A HARRIED facet of time. It does not represent the constancy of longitudinal time, but instead is a reckless gauge. In the large picture of time, speed contains its own irrational laws. It has always carried with it a certain aspect of risk. Nature has its seasons, growth has its gestation period, and the human pulse has its norm. To rush any of them is to invite trouble, and on occasion, disaster.

The need for speed is not brought about by some outer, unrelated influence. We create this need ourselves. Something within us demands haste. Some internal biological craving demands speed.

The history of civilization since the invention of the wheel has been on an accelerated course, picking up speed as it rushes forward. I've often been amused as I've sat in airports, listening to people bitch about delays. Forty minutes late in crossing the country, when it took the pioneers months to reach the Pacific. Of course, that's me. I still don't believe I'm talking to Europe when I call Paris. I'm still awed by television. I often wonder what the human race has done to deserve the ice maker. What drives human beings onward I've grown to understand; but what makes them driven makes me pause and wonder. Somehow getting there seems to be the purpose and getting there quicker is the motivation.

One year in the late '50s, Alwin Nikolais and I toured France and had the special privilege of visiting Lascaux cave. The cave was not yet a popular touring place, and finding it was a chore. The

107

directions we got from the locals were obscure and grudging. Outsiders were beginning to invade this tight mountain community, and they were not welcome. However, we did find the small road leading to the site, paid the nominal entrance fee, and began to tour with four or five others. Since that time, the cave has been closed and a replica created because the air was becoming contaminated. Fungus, bacteria, and mold were beginning to form on the walls, and the fear of loss prompted the French government to protect this mighty antiquity. To see the original cave, to be part of its presence, was an experience that overshadowed the effects of Stonehenge, Chartres, and the Acropolis, for it bypassed the senses and struck directly to bone marrow.

Recorded history began roughly about 7,500 years ago, and Homo sapiens appeared roughly 500,000 years ago, so this prehistoric creation was probably achieved about 15,000 years ago. About 10,000 generations have passed since its creation. I use these generalized figures to find a starting point, to map the acceleration of Western art through the years. Ten thousand years passed before the next great advancement of Mesopotamia and Egyptian art. The skills and materials of art inched forward slowly. The Greeks and Romans followed 2,500 years later. A thousand years afterwards saw the flowering of the great Romanesque and Gothic cathedrals. Four hundred years passed before the paint and canvas of the Renaissance swept the West. One hundred and fifty years later, Impressionism threatened realism. But it was in the 20th century that the acceleration of civilization took off. Music, painting, dance, architecture, science, medicine, social reform, inventions, communications, economics, and every aspect of life speeded up. The great library of Alexandria in Julius Caesar's time contained the staggering collection of 400,000 manuscripts. Today 50,000 new books and periodicals are published every year in the US alone.

Impressionism, expressionism, cubism, fauvism, surrealism, abstract-expressionism, hard-edge, pop, all of these styles raced along under the adrenaline of the speed of communications. What once took hundreds of years to influence civilization can today be disseminated with the switch of a television dial. But dissemination and digestion are two different things. There are some things that cannot be absorbed too quickly without bad aftereffects. Forced growth can be fatal to some organisms. The human body is such an entity. Muscular growth and stretch cannot be forced.

Their development must be measured. Mental growth, however, can be accelerated.

For some reason, probably because it is imperceptible, evolution seems as remote to us today as our great-grandfathers' starched collars. We cannot fathom that we are still evolving. If our bodies cannot change with lightning speed, our minds can. Our inner beings do not all have the same time sense or stretch capacity as do our muscles.

The eye can see and make an instant impression, but to feed that impression into the depths of our senses and soul takes time. Superficially scanning the horizon and visiting a zoo is vastly different from going on a two-week hike and becoming a naturalist. Allowing things to unfold in their own time demands a patience that speed does not contain.

As we rush along compelled by the craving for speed, parts of us will go unnourished and recede and other parts of us, the brain particularly, will shape our evolution along dominant traits.

This is a serious problem for dance because the development of a dancer's skill, which makes for the dance art, cannot be rushed. Muscles and maturity can be stretched only so much and so fast. Speed has its effect on audiences, dancers, choreographers, and ambition. Everything in dance has felt its influence.

Audiences must get out of the theater sooner. A very respectable viewing time today is less than two hours. An hour and forty is preferable. Twenty years ago, a program didn't dare be less than two-and-a-half hours long. The viewing span of audiences has been decidedly altered. Perceptions are keener and the constant visual bombardment of television images has inured us to quicker image reception. The contemporary eye sees more and registers less, because response cannot be rushed.

The average age of dancers comprising a company is getting younger and younger, and with their youth comes formidable technical skills. With this, unfortunately, comes an earlier burnout. I always thought that artistry meant maturity. I learned it still does, but I also learned that maturity has nothing to do with age. Keats, Raphael, and Schubert passed away before what we would consider their mature years, but they nevertheless created from depth.

Dance creators, dance choreographers are the ones who are having the most pressure put on them. The press has whipped them to a frenzy in the race to outdo each other. However, the body of material that has grown most has been the investigations into the craft itself. Its principles, its nature, its substance have all been expanded considerably. Added to this is the abnormal number of people who call themselves choreographers and who crowd the limited grazing ground.

Most new choreographers come to the profession today with a healthy intuition and very limited skills. This is a very frail combination, a very weak balance. Choreography is still 90 percent craft and 10 percent intuition. Putting into movement artistic insight constitutes what an audience sees and what a dancer can cope with. Speed tends to forsake training and experience, and stress popular pressure. This is not negligence on the choreographer's part. It is the nature of the profession. Studying past works may not be available to the choreographer as it is to musicians, writers, and painters. Decent records, or often any records of past masterpieces, are not available to young choreographers. They often must learn from their peers. A dubious challenge, to say the least.

The dance today faces a great many stresses because it is playing into the hands of speed. But then again, how can we ever hope to deal with the vast accumulation of knowledge and art mankind has produced unless we find shortcuts to absorb it?

When I began my training as a dancer, it took seven years for me to master my craft. Today, not only do we know so much more, but we have half the training time to learn it. In addition, the definition of dance changes so whimsically and so arbitrarily that dancers hardly know what they are preparing for. They are pressed to make their success quickly, or they will be left behind.

Why has speed become so enveloping? Because of money and reward. With the new scene comes new heroes, new opportunities, and new successes, however shallow the victories and instant the crowns. They are, nevertheless, symbols of arrival. Like a scythe, speed cuts down the fields of last year's heroes to make room for the new ones.

The dance is not immune to the sweet smell of success, and no one appreciates success more than youth.

Speed is a short ration of time. Who has the time to read Thackeray today, or spend an hour savoring Botticelli? Certainly the time is still there as it always has been, but our genes now have become impatient with taking that time. We are not the 19th-century organisms we once were. Nor can the world afford leisure as it once did. It's a roller coaster of events we live in today. The highs are higher and the lows lower as we rush up and down towards the ultimate destination. How much is being lost in that rush? Should anyone be responsible for the loss? Who are the people responsible for this profession anyway?

The modern dance began in this century. Will it enter the 21st century having outstripped itself?

It would be easy to say, "what's the rush?" if we weren't always being elbowed aside. But art today functions on a fiscal timetable. Everything must be crowded into the annual report. The money that feeds creativity holds the whip. If biological development is dictated by environment, then certainly money has become the artist's environment. The platitudes that art will always have its way despite money is unrealistic. Every artist seeks recompense for his or her labor; I'm sure that the artists of Lascaux were rewarded somehow.

Speed is the route to quick results and quick recompense. Speed means traveling light. It means dumping excess baggage and the burden of history. It means going the path of the short-term future.

One curious thing is that speed has not been abated by the fact of our new-gained longevity. It's understandable that a fruit fly has to accomplish its life cycle in what seems minutes, but with a life expectancy of eighty years looming before us, what's the rush? Money? Fame? Success? Glamour? Prestige? Power? Are these the luscious fruits of the new Garden of Eden? And, if so, what can get us there faster than speed?

Little Man (1953). Alexander Leber

Change

WRITING ABOUT AN ART is difficult. Writing about an artist is impossible. Facts explain themselves. Realities can be seen, but values and motivations are inscrutable and unexplainable and often irrational. The complexity of the mind, the emotions of the muscles are so staggering that they cannot be seen or judged together. Nowhere is this more evident than in the art of performing and in the identity of the performer. This interaction that defines personality defies analysis.

Artists spend their lives securing their work, thinking it will be part of the future, but unfortunately upon completion it becomes part of history. No one secures the future. The dream to do so is a fatal flaw. To do so would only extend the past and arrest growth.

Every living thing, through either instinct or will, wants its presence to be recognized. The dawn chorus is a time when every bird checks in with nature and answers its roll call. The cry of every child as it enters the world is its first defiant statement of self.

The future is always waiting to be born. Artists must face the birth pains of constant rebirth if they are to deal with the future, and birth pains hurt and are often bloody.

Artists seek their identity by creating. They piece their life together with their work. Hopefully a portrait will emerge, because this is the portrait that will live after them. This is how they will be remembered, by their work.

If there is any lesson the wisdom of maturity brings, it is that everything changes, nothing stands still. When I began my career, everything and every place was "for the first time," fresh, eager, exciting, and exhilarating. But on the second and third go-rounds, revisiting cities, playing familiar theaters again, relating to new audiences, I could feel how things had changed. Not for the worse, mind you, but changed. At first this seemed confining because some of the changes seemed unaccountable, until I realized that I was also changing. My perspective never remained the same. My sensibilities had led me to only momentary conclusions. Performance would change from night to night.

Dance is the most ephemeral of all the arts because it exists only with the actual doing. It records itself with bits and pieces. Unless it is actually seen and experienced, its recounting is only a facsimile of the real thing. Even in performance, audience and performer rarely share the same experience. The audience-artist connection is so volatile, so illusive, so immediate, and yet so potent.

There once was a time when all I as a dancer had to worry about was keeping in shape and keeping warm. There once was a time when all choreographers had to worry about was creating and having the time to think about their work. But today that is no longer the case. My crude definition of dance was muscles and bone. But as I danced, taught, and created, I slowly uncovered layer upon layer of internal existences, and as I worked I confirmed and strengthened their identity.

There is no doubt that there are several personalities housed in and comprising our persona: the spirit, the intuition, the emotional, the physical, the sentient, the soul, the moral, the consonant, and others, all working concurrently and often at cross-purposes with each other. The practicing artist is one of the very few people who employs them at the same time. Physiologists, psychologists, and theologians have all staked out their claim and have tried to describe some of them, but only in the nonverbal world of art have they been seen as a unit. It has been during performing and creating that I have touched upon these many existences and understood them as realities and tried to bring them into some coherent balance.

Binding everything with its overwhelming encompassment is time itself. Weaving its own web, tracing its own impervious path. Unconcerned and mocking the trivia of a single lifetime. Time has a particular understanding of design and order. It recognizes when change is necessary and weaves its epochs accordingly.

There is a test used in basic chemistry called the litmus test. A paper impregnated with the litmus dye turns blue in a base solution and red in acid. There need be only one drop to swing the solution to either base or acid and turn the color of the paper from blue to red.

Change is very much like the litmus test. Somewhere along the line, a single potent drop starts the alteration. Most eras and epochs have clean demarcations: war, royal marriage, death. These draw the lines. Governments start and end with election days or coups, but when exactly art starts to redefine itself is all too elusive a process to record.

Art historians who enjoy the dating game try desperately to keep their catalogs in order. I don't know how they do it, especially when you consider that every successful artist influences every other artist. There is no getting away from it. Creativity does not spring full-blown like Venus. It is cross-pollinated on earth. There is no such thing as creative demarcation.

The awareness of change is more a dawning sensation. One becomes aware that what was once high style has taken on an edge of ludicrousness and has become camp. What was once inventive now appears old hat. I see values being substituted everywhere: sterility for passion, physicality for energy, surfeit for selection. One is unsure when the transistor and chip replaced the fuse and tube. When did the microwave replace the gas jet? Suddenly, even the dancers' bodies look different. Change is always heralded with reluctance and then adopted eagerly.

One of the quiet miracles that nature performs is her rejuvenation of the entire cellular system of the body. Roughly every seven years we are remade, and with that reworking comes automatic change. If we were to record lists of personal likes and dislikes and review them seven years later, how we have unconsciously changed would be startling.

When a dancer or any strongly motivated person trains physically and aesthetically for a period of seven years, with a continual consciousness of how he or she wants the body to function, meaning stretch and turnout and vertical awareness, the data banks that are locked into the cells will reprogram themselves. At the end of seven years, the body, which thinks for itself, will automatically adapt to the new data as the norm, and what was once awkward at initial training will become second nature. Even subtle coloration

115

nuance will accompany the change, which for a performing artist frees the mind from having to be conscious of the choreography, script, and score, and lets it give more attention to interpretation.

Change is inevitable. It is not biological growth or development. I speak of the change that makes us differ from our past preferences. It is this change of choice that allows us to cushion our adaptation to the often quixotic course of society. Change is the norm in nature.

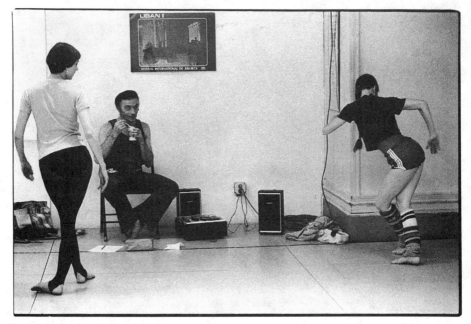

In the Studio (c. 1977). Shostak

Rehearsals

THE STAGE EVENT IS significantly bound at both ends. What happens before the curtain rises and what happens after the curtain falls are equally important parts of a dancer's life. So much is made of the stage performance because this is what everyone sees, this is what the public pays for. The show's the thing. What an audience is less familiar with is what precedes the curtain going up, and what directly follows its descent.

The greatest part of a professional performer's life is spent in rehearsal rooms, not the classroom, and if it is not spent there, then one has not yet become a professional dancer. It is a fine line, but it is one way of determining a professional.

Classrooms and rehearsal rooms are two very different places. Their purpose and intent make them different and also demand separate attitudes. Although physically the room is often the same, once the class is over, rehearsal changes the purpose of the environment radically, as it does the dancers' attitudes. The dancers can no longer leave the class in the hands of the teacher; now their own professional responsibility takes over. Their perceptions, reactions, and output are self-determined. There is no longer the teacher to beat and cajole them; they are on their own.

In no way does the attitude of the classroom prepare dancers for the actual stage performance. In class, the dancers' motivation is limited. They practice steps without much participation unless they are goaded on by the teacher. But in rehearsal all this changes; here they practice their own assertion.

Not every dancer is willing to undergo this responsibility and challenge. There are students in every school who are content to spend almost all of their time taking classes. Neither their ability nor their initiative has ever taken them beyond the classroom. They are known as professional students. The studio has become a home, a solace for them; no longer a point to venture out from, but rather a secure arrival for an indefinite stay. They are happy this way. Their purpose has not been tainted by ambition. The class is their achievement.

Professional dancers know that dancing for their own pleasure is only a part of their commitment. The larger picture includes communication with the audience, getting the message across, delivering. This is practiced in the rehearsal room. Rehearsals constitute about 70 percent of a dancer's schedule. It seems there is never enough time to rehearse new things and always too much time once they are learned.

The drudgery factor appears very early in rehearsals. Slogging through repetitions becomes a way of life. There is always someone screwing up, which means doing it over again and again.

What a dancer develops most is endurance. Normally hot and hasty comes to mind with these volatile people but, much to the contrary, their days are filled with a plodding repetition.

Because every dancer has his or her own particular way of memorizing movement, rehearsals are inconsistent. Some dancers memorize movement slowly, others quickly. Some must memorize in their brains, others in their muscles. Some cannot unlearn and learn choreographic changes quickly, others pick up and drop movements effortlessly. But regardless of this wide discrepancy of rehearsal abilities, a company eventually pulls together and pulls it off. The dance grows in accuracy and quality. Innumerable details are discovered and worked out. Placements, adjustments to different-sized stages, changes in casts, lifts, transitions, each rehearsal cleans and combs the choreographic structure until the dance comes through and begins to shine and become legible. But not without the persistence of rehearsal and the patience of its dreary routine. The rehearsal studio is the scene of both the worst and the most glorious moments in a dancer's day.

It is here that the first great fusion of dance and dancers takes place. Later, onstage, the audience will join them to bring out the best in both dance and dancer. But before performance comes rehearsal after rehearsal.

Because rehearsals are so draining of the psyche, dancers arrive armed with whatever spiritual armor they can muster. High on the survival list is protective clothing. The practice clothes dancers wear for rehearsals is a portrait of each dancer's personality. There is no greater insight into their nature than how they dress themselves for these vulnerable hours. The comfort and solace of these familiar garments is the dancers' only protection against the emotional and physical toll of endless output. Another important thing about practice clothes is their smell. There are times when dancers will bury their heads into a sweater or sweatshirt and nurse themselves through a moment of grief or frustration. I seem to have many of these moments. My sense of smell has grown quite acute. I also think my nose has grown longer.

After this is the way the clothing feels and fits. All dancers share these concerns. Some prefer neat, coordinated rehearsal clothes, while others prefer to wallow in yardage. The worn-and-torn, holes-and-runs look that distinguishes the old "pro" is a little like the old "tar's" sailor hat: beaten and molded to settle on the head at the saltiest angle and, without a doubt, cherished personal gear. The clothes are warm and familiar and hopefully convenient to get out of quickly when going to the "john."

There are also some practice clothes that have been divinely endowed with memory and muscular recall. They, of course, are truly treasured garments. These clothes were worn when a role was first created and are impregnated with all the early imagery and motivation of the choreographer. Putting them on can automatically recall the vividness of the original creative motivation. They are truly magical and greatly revered.

Rehearsals are divided into two parts. The first is the creation or re-creation of a work. The second is learning and rehearsing it. Both involve more than dancing. They demand the skill of being able to wait. Overcoming the strain of waiting, sitting around, getting cold, boredom, daydreaming, falling asleep, and other drains on a dancer's limited spirits is what a professional dancer must contend with and master.

While a ballet is being restaged or newly choreographed, there is nothing dancers can do but wait their turn. In the creation of a new work especially, when the choreographer is already a mass of nerves and the pendulum of curtain time draws the razor's edge closer and closer, knowing how to wait and still offer alert participation is the professional's duty. It is a common sight to see the sides of a rehearsal room draped with bodies waiting their turn. At one time, rehearsals were open-ended affairs. Today they end at an appointed time. This creates pressure for the choreographer, but relieves it for the dancer. Knowing when the waiting will end helps get a dancer through it.

Keeping muscles warm during rehearsals is the dancer's problem, and a great challenge it is indeed. A dancer may be called upon at any moment to get up and dance full out. These sudden contrasts of relaxation and high output are dangerous. Choreographers and regisseurs are not heartless when they make this demand. They have no choice. These rehearsals may very well be the only time they will see the work before it is performed on stage. It is the only time they can control their work. Once the work is onstage, it is completely out of their hands and in the laps of audiences and critics, to be judged or enjoyed or made a plaything. The pressure is intense. The tension or ease of a rehearsal room is determined by the stress on the choreographers or their assistants. Dancers must know how to "go with it" and not feel abused if they are insulted and criticized. Wounded feelings heal faster than injured legs, most of the time.

During these periods of waiting, the dancers are continuously stretching and warming up. Some choreographers find this annoying. The movement is distracting and they feel the dancers' concentration is not focused on the work. They feel the dancers are getting restless and silently complaining about not being used, and in a way, this is all true. But dancers have to move, and there is no controlling their compulsions. While waiting, dancers need to feel out those special parts of their bodies while they stretch. Some pains are worrisome, some are delicious, some remind you of what you did yesterday, and others are warnings of tomorrow.

But the best pains are the tight muscles, because now you know where to work, and how to work. The opening of the hips, the stretching of the muscles, and the ease that comes with it, are the sweet sensual delights of the incessant warming up.

Warming up day after day, year after year, can create mental twinges because of the idiocy of the repetition, so that anything, especially a nudge from a harmless tight muscle, is a welcome and necessary distraction during the daily discipline. At least for that moment you know what you're doing, rather than just doing what you know you should be doing, which in rehearsals is usually waiting.

Some choreographers are sometimes put in a curious position, especially if they are dealing with new talents, young arrivals. Youth is a bloom. It is the first extravagant rose of summer, so fresh, so fragrant, so fulsome, and so fearless. Youth has nothing more to offer than the joy of itself, which is indeed a richness. To harness its wild rapture, to curb its touching belief, to place the first doubt, the first care on that unwrinkled forehead is not a pleasant position to be in, and compassionate choreographers make some consideration for it.

There is a stage in the dancers' development when their technical ability becomes impressive, impressive not only to an audience who sees only that, but to the dancers themselves who feel this sense of accomplishment. The body moves fluently and with assurance. It is that seductive stage of facility. It takes years to arrive at this level, and after years of hard work and discipline, it is understandable that the dancer should want to pause and revel a bit in his or her accomplishment.

But facile is not fulfillment, it is only a fluent description of structure. It is agonizing for dancers to realize that, after attaining this performing level, they must reach up to a still greater height, to sound out their depth. How long will the next stage take? How much more to be sacrificed? Will it be painful?

When a dancer arrives at this facile level, I will say: "Stay awhile, but only awhile. Enjoy the fruits, you've worked for it, you deserve it. Refresh yourself with approval and applause, but prepare yourself to go on. What you achieved was not the goal, only the means to reach the goal."

The goal is artistry, transcendence. OK? Now let's do it again. It is easier with an athlete whose muscles are attached to the bone, but with the dancer they are attached to the soul. They penetrate the memory banks.

Rehearsals are primarily concerned with the creation, execution, and revelation of the choreography. The time spent and the care taken are all directed towards this goal. Any choreography will look poor if it is poorly danced, if it is thinly performed and rambling, if there is no performance intelligence behind it.

Performing intelligence simply refers to knowing what the performers' responsibilities are. Phrasing, texture, music, motional musicality, quality, dynamics, whip, bite, release, emotional flavor, and the whole gamut of sensory responses are the things professionals must learn and provide on their own.

But when things are going well, when the choreography is working and the dancers are bringing it to life, the rehearsal room is heaven, for then they can perform full out, without fear of the consequence of stage mistakes. Both the ease and intensity of performance mix and flow without tension. They push themselves. If they fall, they fall. It doesn't matter.

Once released of the responsibility of stage errors, the dancers become fearless and supremely indulgent. Ease and challenge mingle seductively, tantalizingly urging each other on to achieve breathtaking fulfillment. It is unfortunate that these moments are kept privy from the audiences, for they surely constitute some of the greatest heights of the art. It is at these times, when the dancers are performing for their peers, that their sensitivity, skill, and artistry can be fully appreciated. When a dancer puts out, there is nothing like the rehearsal performance.

Junk Dances (1964). Jack Mitchell

Dressing Rooms

ALMOST ALL OF THE day that is meaningful to dancers is spent in the dressing room, on the stage, in the wings, and in the rehearsal hall; what little is left hopefully is spent in bed. The needs and the functions of society are somehow sifted around these places. Onstage, they play the perfectionist, and on the road they play for keeps, because it is a killing game.

Usually when you are on tour and enter a dressing room for the first time, the first thing to do is drop your heavy carryall bag on the dressing table, look around the room, and start bitching. I said usually, not always. I have on occasion arrived at wonderful quarters where the pleasure of complaint was frustratingly stilled. The color of the walls, hideous, and those drapes, a ghastly blue (or red or yellow or whatever may be hanging there). Note: Be careful not to waver in your discontent if the color is appealing, otherwise you are out; you lose.

No hangers, a single bulb hanging from the ceiling directly behind your back that lights your sideburns and ears. Leaking taps or no water, or an air-conditioning system with a guiding instinct to reach you no matter where you are in the room, and the usual throbbing muscle grinch, under your left shoulder blade, from the long bus ride is honing your instinct to seek out all the other discomforts.

There is a bareness about touring dressing rooms that has a chilling character of its own. Too many people have been here

127

before. The dressing tables are marked with wounds. The sparse and crooked hangers dangle mournfully, exhausted at the thought of yet another costume to hang from their already defeated shoulders. The abused furniture is too discouraged to offer anything but itself as a shabby welcome. But by the evening the transformation is remarkable. The room for the next few hours will have an identity: yours.

The performer's magic of purpose is undaunted. Even with these tiresome intrusions of dreary quarters, one sweep and a suite appears, furnished, flamboyant, and fostering. A pumpkin into a coach; even more impressive, a purse without a sow's ear.

Whatever obstacles a dressing room may offer, it is still home for the time the dancer must use it, and home it becomes. Telegrams and photographs line the mirror. Candles are lit. Fetishes are unpacked and spaced about. Trinkets are hung, the kitchen laid out, and makeup, tissues, hair dryer, and other essentials find their places; costumes, clothing, and rehearsal clothes decorate the walls.

To a sponsor, any space can be called a dressing room. Anything into which a table and chair can be crammed warrants the name. Closets, niches, alcoves can all be elevated to rooms if the purpose need only be to serve a performer (bitch, bitch).

Some people can function to capacity in small spaces, others unfortunately don't. The size of a dressing room and the available space within it is vital to the well-being of the performing organism. Not only is it important to surround the physical body with room enough to stretch out, but one must be careful not to crowd the psyche as well.

The aura surrounding a personality can be of considerable power. Strong personalities move out into the space around them. They need to occupy double and triple portions of space and, if that space is compressed or pinched and the performers cramped or thwarted, aside from headaches and grouchiness, they evidence other nasty symptoms no one really cares to be near.

Some dressing rooms are placed convenient to the stage, while, with others, the distances are so great, the dancers have time to review all their counts before they reach the wings, which sometimes is fortunate because often it is the only rehearsal dancers may have of the role they are performing that evening. ("But we rehearsed this only last week, don't you remember?")

128

In America, permanent dressing rooms are a luxury. So few dancers have permanent jobs. In opera houses, they are assigned according to status. The stars get the coziest nests. In large professional theaters, they are well-appointed and impressive, but in many other theaters, they present nothing more than the tawdry evidence of misuse.

The Paris Opéra offers a paragon of dressing rooms (loges). The rooms are divided between singers and dancers. The singers get the first choice. Here an *étoile* may live as long as twenty years in the same quarters. The artists themselves design and refurbish their rooms—at their own expense, of course—and the style of interior decor has a wide range. From silvered walls to palm trees, beaded curtains to heavy velour draperies, rugs, divans, and chandeliers are visible, and in many, the most astonishing mess of heaped clothing.

In America, the term "dressing room" covers an impressive variety of spaces. In addition to some very fine quarters in good theaters, there are the public-school kindergarten rooms with their diminutive kiddy-sized furnishings. Part of all professional dancers' experience includes applying makeup with their knees under their chins and a mirror resting on a baby's table yards away from their faces. Some dressing rooms seem to be designed for standees where, once a chair is brought up to the table and the performer sits on it, he or she finds the chin resting on the tabletop and the head below the vision of the mirror. I usually handle this by letting my head rest on the table for about five minutes as my life passes in review.

One purpose of the dressing room is to serve as a dining room, although the fare does not usually constitute a large menu. There are the biscuits and cookies that range from the sober tea biscuit to the addiction-related chocolate cookie. Note: Eating the hellish nut-topped chocolate-covered marshmallow cookie, once started, cannot be stopped. Keep away from them. They are death.

Tea is found on the kitchen corner of the dressing table. An electric hot water pot is surrounded by a thermos, cup and saucer, and sugar or honey. The cutlery consists of a Swiss army knife and a spoon. Coffee is brought in from outside or is a gift from the stage crew's coffee pot.

Candies abound. Chocolate heads the list, milk or bittersweet, with or without nuts, but always the thick kind. Boxed chocolates go all too quickly. All visitors seem to feel it their duty to relieve you of a couple of them. Chewy and fudge, creams and caramels, mysteriously wrapped or blatantly alluring, they nourish the compulsions and irrational anxieties brought about by waiting. They are consumed by the pound, and yes, yes, yes, dancers know how bad it is for them to eat the stuff, but God, are they necessary.

Fruit is important to get the tart and fresh taste of nature back into your mouth after the dirt and tension of the stage has dried you out.

It is usual for dancers to nap or rest before performances. Ideally, this should be done in the dressing room. But when two or more dancers share a room, this becomes difficult because of everyone's varied timetable for preparation, so off they all go to find different quarters for their naps. When they are not in use, the floors of the stage, lobbies, aisles, orchestra pit, costume room, and other quiet places soon become dormitories as everyone beds down.

When the dressing table turns into a desk, letters are written here upon the elegant and impressive stationery taken from fine hotels at which one occasionally stays. Business matters are also discussed with the surprising number of managers who seem to appear after every performance, some offering you experience, others instant discovery and room and board for a one-nighter somewhere on Lake Como.

The dressing room is also the place for the last warmup before going onstage. With makeup applied, the dancers put on a warm outfit and go through that last personal preparation to reassure themselves that their legs are still working, their backs still bending, their strength is still there. This warmup is more to placate anxieties, and it also brings a glow of moisture to the makeup, which blends it to the face for a soft luminosity. Costumes are applied last to avoid perspiration stains and wrinkling.

Then there are also those nightmarish moments when, before a concert as one reviews counts at the dressing table, choreographic blackouts occur. "What followed that arm movement, and which leg took the turn?" Absolute blank. More than fear, there is confusion as to why the memory lapse should have occurred, especially because the part was well-rehearsed and often performed. I no longer let those moments worry me, because I know that once onstage both the memory and the muscle recall will remember everything, and I'll laugh and say, "How the hell could I have forgotten that?" I had forgotten that the memory remembers and the muscles recall.

130

The onstage call comes, and as the dancers leave the dressing room there is a sense of security. They know that they will return to this room. They know that, whatever happens on that stage, there is still this place, this haven, this nest, this retreat, this dressing room to which they will return afterwards in triumph if all goes well, or dismay if it doesn't. In the endless chaos of dancers' lives, the dressing room becomes a security blanket. If not the dressing room, at least the makeup table, because they leave their personal identity there, to be reclaimed later when the makeup is removed.

Entre-Acte (1959). Susan Schiff Faludi

Makeup and Costumes

As CURTAIN TIME APPROACHES, so does the time of transformation, and then the dressing room finds its real purpose: making up.

Painting the face, as in the Indian Kathakali dances, can take as many as six hours as layers of applications dry. The makeup ritual is a very personal ceremony. Each performer has his or her own discipline for application.

First, the makeup is arranged in special ways upon the table: brushes, pencils, liners, colored greases, pancake, mascara to be mixed with water or spit as the case may call for. All become a palette for change.

Then from the mirror, two cautious and wary eyes appear to direct the transformation. The performer emerges. His or her judgment and awareness quickly wipe out any pedestrian intrusion. Squinting, straining, judging, those potent eyes guide every line, every application. The ritual begins, the making up starts.

The most important part of this transformation will be to create a new housing for the eyes. Eyes that are often faded, sleep-ridden, and lensed soon find a new definition and a new strength. Lines extend the eyes out, bringing with them a wider vision as well as greater depth, replacing the common shallowness of ordinary seeing. The lines surrounding the eyes make a portal through which the soul of the new character can emerge.

Witch doctors of old painted lines and colors upon their faces to gain admission to strange and holy inner places. Through their eyes, they contacted the spirits of the air, and through their feet, they spoke to the earth. The metamorphosis of paint revealed a womb from which emerged a gamut of beings, earthly as well as ghostly. Today characters of all sorts still appear: heroes and crones, villains with misshapen hearts and noses, as well as the vapid perfections of pallid princesses.

Noses, the most visible part of the face, are restructured, lengthened, straightened, curved, or shortened. The mouth is hardened or softened, made fuller or crueler, sensual or covered. Every vestige of the person is tampered with, and when the makeup is completed, a very different person rises from that table and assumes command. Chilling in authority, assured and elegant, nothing like that somewhat reluctant and bedraggled individual who earlier entered the dressing room. A new creature rises and heads for the ceremonial ground, the stage.

Along the walls, drowsing and airing, the costumes hang. The street clothes, hanging a little self-consciously nearby, exaggerate the difference between the two personalities that split the inhabitant of the room. The costumes are clearly for this time and this place, waiting lifelessly for the performer to fill them. Waiting for the dressing room to incubate that life.

Costumes have a history of their own. The skin we were born with was our original costume, and after eighteen years of stretching and reshaping, losing and gaining, it finally fitted to contain us. Fortunately not all costumes take as long to fit. Costumes from their earliest use were a means of disguise. Whereas clothing functioned to warm and beautify the figure, costumes gave one another identity.

Although witch doctors, the direct ancestors of the performer, had profound and important things to divine and prophecy, they knew that as actors they were going to be more effective if they dressed the role. When dealing with the creatures of the earth, they found that these creatures were more responsive if they were recognized as one of their own. Furs, skins, and feathers became matters of soul and spirit, darkness and night. They designed their costumes symbolically.

Tribes and audiences soon came to recognize the costumes and the characters that they represented. Here was the rainman and this the deer. That was the moon and this was someone who crept about at night and ran off with your soul as you lay sleeping, especially if your mouth was open.

But when the great theater of religion split in two, in order to clarify the domain and power between the secular and the spiritual, the secular claimed the double world of reality and make-believe, while the spiritual inherited the soul and the hereafter. One built theaters, and the other churches, and both worried about filling their houses.

From the earliest years of childhood the easiest way to create make-believe was to paint your face and dress up. The more outlandish, the more the make-believe. Every kid knows that, and every performer knows what every kid knows.

Motley, "a thing of rags and patches," became a uniform, an identification. The Italian mummers formalized the domino costume and added masks to their faces to establish the characters of *commedia dell'arte.*

The current fashions of the day became acceptable for onstage wear as well as offstage, and, in the 18th century, Shakespeare's Antony and Cleopatra would languish seductively in Restoration frills. Louis XIV brought together high French fashion with theater costume design for an outrageously garish encounter.

It wasn't until the 19th century that a costume designed solely for dancing came about as did other wonders of theatrical make-believe during the Romantic period. Music, dance, and dramatic stagecraft converged into a theatrical flowering to release the viewer's imagination, leaving the advancement of facts to the new sciences.

The tutu, as we know the fluffy gauze garment today, first started long, went up, then stuck out, and finally settled for a flexible length. The Greek tunic design, intended to drape and show the contours of the body, was made of a little heavier fabric. The sheath had a starker look and emphasized the whole torso.

The leotard was a full-body garment worn by a French acrobat, Léotard. Through its long and baggy history, it finally emerged as the elastic clinging basic costume for the dancer. Stretch fabric changed more than the look of the dancer's costume. It changed the dancer's body as well. Now every body part was highly visible as a result of the skintight fit. Every protrusion drew attention. Breasts, bulges, and backsides were very evident, and the long leggy look emerged. Tulle, tutu, and tunic saw their day, and were relegated to the world of classical dance.

Ballet performers live in a world of special roles. As actors and actresses place Juliet, Romeo, Lady Macbeth, and Hamlet on a dais in the pantheon of the theater, so do ballet dancers their Giselle, Albrecht, Odette, and James. There are about a dozen such roles that are the embodiment of all the years of ballet history. Ballet artists dance these parts where and whenever they can. This traveling employment is called "guesting," a gracious term that means an invitation to appear with a host company. The artists for these engagements usually supply their own costumes. These are very special costumes for dancers, and they are usually sewn with great care and love.

These costumes are an important link to the mystique of the art. Although the costume is for a standard character, the costumes themselves are filled with a great deal of individuality. Cut, design, trimming, and fabric are all dealt with very personally.

One evening a mutual friend of Nureyev's and mine invited us both to dinner. This friend had rented Rudolf's home in London, and it was curious to see Rudolf roam through his own house as a guest. After dinner, which was a very nervous affair because Rudolf had reversed the roles and made the hosts feel like guests, we went upstairs to see the rest of the house. While checking out this floor, I found myself standing next to him as he opened a closet door. I looked where he looked, and my eyes opened wide, for there hung the costumes he had worn during his fantastic career. There must have been twenty of them. I stood quietly and watched as he walked into the closet, lifted a protective cover from them, and stared. He leafed through them one by one. "What," I thought, "must be going through that mind?" Those weren't just costumes he was sorting. They were more than memories. They were the very pages of his life. It was almost as if one thumbed through a catalog of triumphs.

He lifted one out, a beautifully detailed jacket, and stared hard at it. He returned it, covered them all, and closed the door. I felt awkward being there, for I had just watched a man review his life, by handling it, hardly a time for spectators.

The most successful costumers are those who can both design and execute the costumes. Designers who only create on paper to a large degree design for themselves, but costumers who can also sew them design for the performer.

One of my great fortunes was to meet and work with Frank

136

Garcia. Frank came into my life twenty-five years ago and has remained an integral part of my work since then. A great costumer understands the final destination of a costume, the stage. He understands its function in a production, and its compatibility with the performer who wears it. To a great extent, costumers must sublimate their talents in favor of purpose and practicality.

Frank's knowledge of what would work was so much a part of his design that there was little time wasted in trial and error. His tactile feeling for fabric and fit is delicious to watch. Of course, on cold days, as his icy hands molded material to a patiently standing chilled body, and his fingernails etched seam lines over breasts and crotches and inner thighs, the dancer begins to realize the sensual basis of costuming. The frozen drab body standing there suddenly senses what parts of the body are going to bring the costume to life; the round of the buttocks, the pelvic bones, the lift of the upper back, the abdomen. A second skin is being formed. The image will soon emerge.

A costume should vividly imply the new character a dancer will step into. It should be able to hang patiently on a rack, coming to life only as warm flesh is poured into it. A costume is an identity waiting to be lived. It is the makeup the body wears.

One of the legendary ladies of the ballet who had gained an enviable reputation for the use of her gifted hands and certain eye was Karinska. There is not one choreographer, designer, or dancer who has worked with her who does not sing her praise. And those wardrobes that are blessed enough to contain her handiwork are blessed indeed.

At the Paris Opéra a recently retired costume director was awarded the Legion of Honor. The present one is also revered and loved. Her costumes are her chicks, and like a warm mother hen she bosses and tends them all affectionately.

The heroes and heroines of the ballet were created from 19th-century romances, and for the men, the short vest jacket design has always maintained a courtly styling. What makes them different today is that they probably fit better. Often in busy opera houses very little care is given to special fittings. There is only time for general alterations, and when the casts are changed with practically every performance, a matinee set of costumes are sometimes delivered, damp with sweat, into the dressing rooms of the evening cast. Art can carry a heavy underarm burden with it.

But not all costumes impart such dubious dignity. In Stuttgart, I watched Marcia Haydée rehearse an appearance in *La Dame aux Camilles* wherein she stood alone onstage for a few minutes draped in a dark, heavy, floor-length fur coat. Of course, she couldn't possibly have lifted a leg with that weight on, but, oh, how it must have lifted her spirits. Later in the rehearsal, I saw the coat flung carelessly across a chair with other bits of discarded costumes thrown upon it, waiting to be collected and returned to wardrobe.

There once was a time when there was no question about the look, both in rehearsal and onstage, that distinguished the modern dancer from the ballet dancer, but today only the bare feet, the tutu, and the princely jacket tell them apart.

Perhaps someday we'll go full circle and return to our first costumes and dance in the nude. Just think, no fittings, no pins, no after-show rinsings, no cleanings, no runs, no broken zippers, only the discoloration of every rehearsal bruise visibly revealed in vivid color, and the texture of goose pimples on the cold nights.

Journal (1957). David Berlin

Performance

PERFORMANCE IS THE ART of doing. It is the enactment of the event. Performance is the world of the performers. In this domain, they join the audience and together they hasten towards the creator's purpose.

Performance is an entity unto itself. It exists in its own right and carries with it its own conditions for existence. It is a culmination that identifies it as a particular entity. The nature of it is fluid and always changing to suit the nature of each event. Its vitality comes from four sources: the physical performers, the artistry that they employ, the choreography they perform, and the audience. Together they produce that entity called performance.

Performance crowns the event. Performance is not mired, it floats. It exists upward, it hovers. It is immediate. It happens. It has no roots, it feeds from the air. It floats above all the tangibles that create it. From its loftiness, its aura descends and permeates all, lifting everything to its height as well as its depth. Performance is the revelation that speaks for itself.

The performing arts rest in black boxes, in scripts, on music sheets, in the memory and the muscles, waiting to be filled with human concern and brought to life. But human concerns are all too variable, too chancy, and irrational. The thermometer of life varies with every passion. The fever of existence both blazes and chills.

Performance is a place that exists only at a certain time. The time is not a set time, but when it is set, then that place exists. And when that time is past, that place is also gone.

There is a gall that sweetens all it sours, sharpening every flavor, heightening every sense. There is a balm that bathes the soothing cutting edge. But when the time is ended, the gall turns bitter again. There is the rage that drenches everything till there is no time and there is no place; all is sublimated.

Surfing through corridors of cresting waves, balancing through the viewers' tenuous tunnels of response, riding the exhilaration of intimacy, is this transport called performance.

With the first dimming of the houselights, the performance begins. Everything quickens. In the audience, conversations rush to conclusions. Anticipation salts everything with excitement.

In the drape-lined canyons of wings, dancers wait, keeping perspiring feet dry, or stretching into shoes. The stage banter continues, but no one is listening much. The ear is stretching to farther frequencies. The placement it took all day to achieve is now slipped into easily. Shoulders, necks, and heads are fussed with like ill-fitting gloves.

With the first sound of the overture, the pulse rises in every limb of the theater. In the dressing rooms, the waiting is over. In the house, it is the last time to adjust coats. In the wings, "they're at the gate."

And then the curtain rises. Like an ogre lifting his single eyelid to stare out, the stage awakens.

Swelling to larger and new proportions, the dancers' energy level increases to vibrancy. The eyes enlarged and feverish, lungs extended, the dancers enter. With the first step onstage, their presence will make every judgment. It is totally in control. It appears as the embodiment of assurance. It allows the audience to relax and know that everything is in control.

Presence is courage. It comes from knowing the role very well or the extraordinary courage to push through six roles you don't know very well. But it is that strength, that ability to grip and control the internal muscles, the muscles that surround and house the will and determination.

For these next hours, the dancers will etch their presence on the spatial canvas of the stage. They will perform. It is the time when little birds put on condor wings. The alertness the dancers will demand of themselves will illuminate their immediacy of being and influence their timing, speed, and brilliance.

142

Immediacy is the ability to arrest the moment of "now" so that an audience can see and partake in the present. It does not allow the dull blade of time to cast its inevitable shadow of the past on the present. The act is vitalized and enlarged, magnifying it out of all proportion and making it dominate its existence. The audience can see nothing else, feel nothing else, and respond only to that which the dancers want them to see.

Of all the performing arts, dance makes the greatest demands upon its audience. Dance must be seen. Its first entree to the viewer is through the eyes. Music and drama rely primarily on sound, and the audience can rest their eyes occasionally and never lose the continuity of the event. But the structure of a dance becomes disjointed if the eye closes or is distracted.

Swelling to enlarged size and proportions, the dancers enter. Understanding the importance of that initial contact and the crucial maintenance of that relationship, the performers exceed their physical boundaries and press closer to the viewer.

Choreographers may say their art is greater than the performers'. The performers may say there is no art without the artist, but in performance, the demarcation of choreography and performance almost disappears. The performers will manipulate this material with such ease that it would seem they created it themselves. The outpouring is uninterrupted. There is no intrusion as to who created what. The audience must be affected by a single sentient line of communication.

If one assumes that the human being consists of a corporeal outer being of flesh and bones and brain, and an inner spiritual being that houses the soul, then the purest dedication of an artist is to nourish that soul.

The performers and the audience bear a very important common line of communication, pulse. Pulse, timing, rhythm, and beat course inevitably through both bodies. The dancers send out long tentacles to grasp firmly the instinct that is housed in the circulation system of the viewer. By controlling the heartbeat of the viewer, they have assured another entree into the identification of their roles. By accelerating that pulse or retarding it to unbearable slowness, the performers can create pleasure, discomfort, excitement, sensuality, and the whole gamut of physical and emotional response, feeding into the viewer the internal nature of motion, thereby assuring communication in and of the abstract.

143

Once the soul has been racked and made vulnerable, the intellectual imagery takes over and floods the mind with associations and memories. These sensations become new input for the memory banks, expanding them both superficially and profoundly.

With the time factor so essential, the dancers are at the double mercy of the conductor or the sound system and their own bodies. If musical tempi are slow, they must extend the movement further into space. If fast, they quickly redistribute the time so that nothing appears rushed or harried, shaving fractions from small movements so that larger extensions can be fulfilled and don't appear cramped.

They make these decisions instantaneously. These reapportionments are further influenced by their metabolism. Dancers have heavy days and nervous days. Both are erratic and dangerous if they aren't fully controlled during performance. If the dependability of the lower spine, the legs, and the abdomen are off that day, then the performing presence must concentrate on those off areas to keep them in balance.

Performing artists are never comfortable onstage. Assured, yes, but the glitter of anxiety is necessary for brilliance. As the performance continues, the ducts of passion open wider and wider until the flood carries the artists along in waves of release. At this point, the power of presence stands guard. Intoxication can mean losing control, and yet everything, everyone must be intoxicated at the same time. The heights and falls and climax are determined by the performing presence.

The artists are fully prepared. They know. Things left to the last moment are generally things inadequately done, excepting, of course, for those moments of inspiration that have no schedule for appearance.

Throughout performance, there are constant distractions; people fussing in the wings, noisy stagehands, parts of costumes becoming undone, a bad placement causing a sudden pain. The whole unpredictable stage life making its unpredictable self known and felt. Intrusions into those tenuous bonds of communication are always happening. But the performers are undaunted. At times, they thrive on the unexpected to enlarge their performing force.

The channels from stage to audience widen, and now the performers can bring the larger blinding light of rapport to focus on anything they choose.

Nuance, subtlety, detail, and delicacy can be illuminated as brilliantly as is the spectacle. The broad and heavy roads of prose have reached the inroads of poetry. Higher and higher, deeper and deeper, the inroads are wide enough only for intimacy. The audience follows helplessly into this bourn.

— Like a painter, the dancers apply coloration to movement through dynamics. Using different brushstrokes to apply energy to the space about them, they turn inward as quickly, to texture the space within. Expanding it, contracting it, hardening, loosening, softening, sharpening, qualifying every motion so that the body always speaks from depth.

The larger physical structure of the dance is its movement structure; performance reveals its internal motional identity.

Throughout the performance, the dancers are focused relentlessly towards their art. They can no longer go backwards, but only forward. They are riding a current. This exhausting concentration must be released occasionally and, during those moments when they can leave the stage, they disappear into those mysterious enclosures at the sides of the stage called wings. Once in these cloistered vantage points, they can wait and watch. Hiding in these spaces, they can prepare for their next entrance. Lips are moistened, costumes adjusted, sweat blotted and wiped off, reality is touched upon momentarily while the body refuels itself. The wings are launching pads, takeoff sites. After one exits gasping from the stage, the lungs can be refilled, noisily hacking and gasping. Everything can be recharged. Characterizations and qualities are dropped immediately, and all concerns shift to the preparation for the next entrance.

Onstage again, there is no reason to confront the audience head-on. Now, if all has gone well, they are willing to be led. The dancers need not press fully out towards the audience, but can operate more obliquely. They can throw their performance to any point onstage or any point in themselves, and channel the audience's full attention away from the self, the personality, the ego. The structure or choreography begins to speak and identify itself. This otherwise lifeless entity is now enlivened by the performers' powers, and one can see the work.

Now in full command, the performers feed and illuminate themselves and the art around them. Traveling this double track, riding first one then the other, they finally step into the time warp of performance and ride them both simultaneously. "Tiene Angel;" they are touched by an angel. They tread the divine.

Revelation is mankind dealing with eternity.

Journal (1957). Seymour Linden

The Curtain Falls

AT THE OTHER END of the performance is the final curtain. Once the stage curtain comes down, the performing world ends, and another flood of sensibilities washes over the dancer. When the curtain is up, the focus is always out to the audience. Once the curtain drops, all feelings revert inward, into the self. It's a confusing moment. There is a terrible sense of severance, a sense of loss. Something has been cut off. One is suddenly alone. With the energy released, the letdown is enormous. Sometimes it is nothing more than a good feeling of exhaustion. It is over. Sometimes it is crushing. Sometimes dancers need to hold each other to make the transition back to the present.

The dancer walks to the wings, weight no longer forward on the toes, chest no longer lifted, hips no longer pressed forward: just a body guided by the homing instinct to get back to the dressing room. Bits of clothing are collected from the wings, leg warmers, robes, towels. Sometimes dressers stand by to do this collecting and lead the dancer off.

If anything went wrong that evening with the performance, the dancers involved will get together and work out the problem while they are still warmed up and are in the performing heat. They'll go over counts or review a supported lift or talk over staging.

But mostly there is the letdown. The relief that the evening is over. The relief in knowing there are now another twenty-four hours to build up to another performance. A resistance to being pushed or hurried anymore sets in, and everything slows down. But if one moves too slowly from the stage, there remains a lurking danger, for suddenly guests appear who know the theater well and can get backstage quickly to greet you, to compliment you, or simply to let you know they are in town. If the conversation goes on for any length of time, others generally appear and surround you. This is an awkward moment because you know you're trapped onstage.

Visitors are compelled to linger backstage. To bring well wishes, silent thanks, respect, and very often just their presence. But they all linger. To absorb, to give mute testament of their love. Most come to bring some form of respect.

If the dancer can make it to the dressing room before guests appear, there is the problem of receiving them in small quarters. There is the problem of getting out of costume and makeup before guests arrive. There is the problem of getting to restaurants before they close. There is the problem of being trapped with makeup half off, and the resultant greenish-gray smear of cold cream and mascara covering your face as you greet people. There is the awkwardness as you rise naked from your chair to greet someone you respect with only a face cloth to cover everything you wished covered. And there is the realization of how quickly you have descended from the heights.

But none of this is as sobering as the disorienting shock when that final curtain drops.

Recently I attended a performance of the Martha Graham Company. Included in the program was *Errand into the Maze*. It was a role in which Graham herself was once absolutely electrifying. After the curtain had dropped, I started backstage to visit someone. By the time I got to the wings, I heard the roar of response from the audience and turned to see Martha onstage. The audience rose and acclaimed her. I stood in the wings and watched. The applause lasted for several minutes, and the final curtain came down.

In a matter of seconds the company disappeared from the stage leaving Graham alone. The great lady stood by herself, a little confused by the suddenness of the ending and being left alone. Since no one was around, I walked towards her. She gave me her hand. I told her how delighted I was to see her.

"Were you pleased with the performance this evening?" I asked.
"Yes, they danced very well."

150

"You know," I said, "I once saw *Errand* danced so breathtakingly by another dancer that I can still remember it vividly today."

She paused for a moment, thought, and looked at me. "Yes, I was rather good, wasn't I?"

There is a rejuvenation that the backstage brings that can instill new life to memories and renew the urgency of the past. When the curtain is up, the present unfolds; when it is down, the stage can re-create memories just as vividly as giving a wakening kiss to the sleeping past.

When the curtain is up, the dancers are swept along with their glorious achievements; when the curtain is down, they can be overcome with the mistakes they made that evening. It would seem that all the dancers remember are the mistakes. Generally they laugh them off, but often they indulge themselves in a bit of self-crucifixion, driving the stakes of error deeper and deeper into themselves, turning a glorious evening into a pit of remorse. In almost every case, the audience never sees any of these "shattering errors."

Vladimir Vasiliev is one of the most beautiful, complete, and stirring performers of our time. I have watched him dance, and I have been transformed. I have also seen him after an incredible performance walk offstage, shaking his head over some imperfection so invisible and so inconsequential, to nurse his dejection. This guilt must come from some sort of insecurity, although dancers call it striving for perfection.

"Spank your child once a day," says a Chinese maxim. "If you don't know what he has done wrong, he does." Performers always know what they've done wrong and will readily confess it to anyone.

There is a belief in this world of performance that no one has ever given a perfect performance, nor ever will. These are the unattainable standards artists set for themselves.

There is another thing that occurs just as the curtain drops. It is a strange phenomenon, made stranger still by the fact that it is very real, physical, and visible. For some reason, cuts, wounds, bruises, and sprains neither appear nor are felt until the letdown after the performance, and then suddenly blood flows, muscles cramp up, and spasms begin. It is really an extraordinary testament to the power of the spirit. The passion of performing is an anesthetic to physical pain.

151

But now with guests gone, makeup off, washed and dressed, you look about and the heartbreak begins. As you're leaving the dressing room, bouquets of lovely fresh flowers remain behind staring at you, confused by your departure, having to say "good-bye" before you've both gotten to know each other.

The dressing room door is closed, and you begin to leave the theater. Sometimes the stage door takes you past the stage. You look in. It is dark, empty, ghostly, stripped.

Once the curtain falls, there is very little you can do but watch as the stagehands brutalize the magic that only moments before filled the stage. In a matter of minutes, the stage is struck and darkened, and everything is gone. Every trace of the work, the beauty, the giving, the response, gone, all gone. And that other world, reality, steps out of the shadows and demands its share of your life. You walk out into the cool night, out into that other world. Gone, all that work gone. And tomorrow, all that work to re-create it again.

A Fine Line (1992). Nan Melville

Conclusions

THE PORTRAIT OF AN artist is painted slowly and with care. It is built up step-by-step upon a canvas. Brushed and dabbed into an identity with stories, speculations, and facts, until a picture emerges. Not of a single dancer but of a semblance of many. Art is not a singular term, it is of the plural. Much has preceded and more will come.

Dancing, like song, is an achievement of man, and man is an achievement of nature. Art links and relates the two. Everything ends. People die, memories fail, merry-go-rounds stop, and curtains fall. But it is only by these conclusions that we understand the beginnings.

The portrait takes its shape. A person emerges, an artist appears, a profession defines itself. Dancers are restless subjects, they cannot sit still and be copied. They do not present only one side of themselves to the world. Sometimes the brilliance of this impression impairs the viewer's vision, and sometimes it is poignantly clear.

Time and triumphs tamper with the dancer's appearance. The triumphs they can control, but time is a wicked host. It has no allegiances, no favorites. It clearly sees what is there, what is inevitable, makes its reckoning, and hurries on. It sees the outline of the next face appear before the portrait is completed. It watches impassively as its cohort, history, is attracted to the emergence of the new face, the flickerings of a new star.

How quickly is the brush lowered from the old canvas and a new

155

palette prepared. How quickly is the next canvas stretched and the next portrait begun.

If there is a price dancers pay to serve their art, it is this: the price of an unfinished portrait.

But dancers are not a passive breed. They outrage social patterns and commit the unforgivable affront, they exalt. They rise above. Like startled larks, early-lifers fly upwards while society trudges forward.

They know who paints the final stroke, who puts the signature to the work, where immortality lies. It is those memories that put the signature to the canvas. The dancer's immortality is assured. It is seared forever into the hearts of those they have claimed. For if they are remembered, they will always live on.

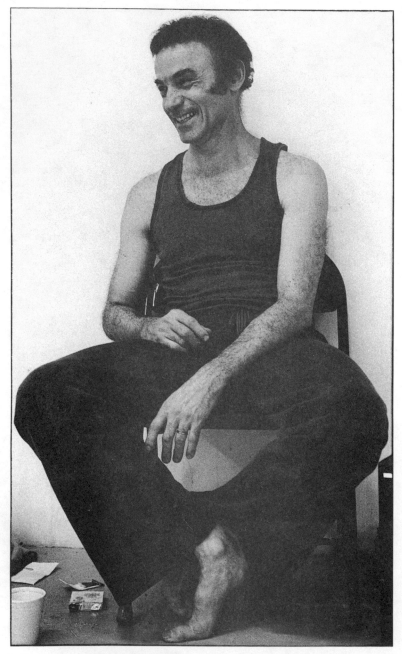

In the Studio (c. 1977). Shostak

Notes to Myself

If you don't know the harmony of both grace and grossness, it is difficult to make judgments.

* * *

When performers set a role they have danced many times on another dancer, they usually set what they think they've danced. That is why it always looks different to the choreographer.

* * *

Choreographing at the Paris Opéra was like playing polo. Rehearsing, changing, correcting while riding a fast steed. Everything was always a race with time.

* * *

My education was limited. My penmanship didn't include handwriting on the wall.

* * *

For a number of reasons, every choreographer has to create a bad work occasionally. This is a great deal more difficult than it may sound.
1. Resentment for being pushed into the responsibility of mounting a work.
2. Boredom.

3. *Perversity to just be lousy.*
4. *A fallow period—very legit for the creative process.*
5. *The privilege of failure.*
6. *It is a necessary catharsis. A cleaning of the senses and of the creative palate.*

* * *

Interested people often don't want you. They are interested in the things they want from you.

* * *

Sometimes when on tour, the alarm clock will go off and waken me. Not only don't I know where I am, I often don't know who I am.

* * *

I've always thought the great question was not—"What is the meaning of life"—but, "Will the sunrise waken us tomorrow?"

* * *

Cats are too self-centered—if the conversation isn't about them, they'll get up and walk away.

* * *

In time, rebels must defend the things they rebelled against.

* * *

One of the definitions of civilization is continuity.

* * *

A comedy is like a soufflé—if you interrupt its critical rising, it will fall.

* * *

The eye begins to taste dinner long before the mouth does.

* * *

I close my eyes more and more often these days because I have seen too much. One talks of the heart, but the heart knows only what the eyes care to show it.

Artists know that the definition of "balls" is commitment.

Modern dance and ballet are basically oil and vinegar. Sometimes you can find a good choreographer who can mix them. But they must be shaken constantly or else they separate very quickly.

The arts differ in the isolation they demand of the creator, from the turbulent gregariousness of the choreographer to the isolation and quiet of the writer.

I think best alone, but surrounded. In train stations, at the theater, movie houses, on streets. While I think, the rest of me can occupy itself watching other things.

I would often sigh those huge sighs that have become so character-istic of me. "It is life," I say. "It often hugs me too tightly."

I have never had an understudy. In my long career it never occurred to me, or for that matter anyone else, that I would ever be unable to perform.

I hate everything. I hate everyone. I don't want to dance. My knee hurts. I don't want to bend my back. I want to be alone. I don't know what I want. I want to cry. I want sympathy. I don't want to push anyone. I don't want to be pushed. I want to go home. I don't want to go home because it's only more headaches. I don't want anyone on my back. I'm tired. I got too much sun today. I can't stand waiting before shows. I'm so bored I could scream. When I scream everyone gets upset. Why the hell couldn't Dvořák write a more suitable last movement? There are flies in my room. I finished a good book, and the new one is depressing. I've got a headache. My coffee was cold this morning, and the cat wouldn't play with me. My rehearsal clothes smell, and I've got a new split on my left foot. I have a feeling all this means I'm getting ready to start choreographing a new dance.

* * *

Even the most original thinking is sparked by someone else's ideas.

* * *

There are times when I am choreographing for a company other than my own, when choreography becomes a charade. I become a tailor of motion. I would sew the steps together and hope the dancers knew how to wear them.

* * *

As the neck of the giraffe reaches to the higher branches, so are our principles stripped of their lower branches as we reach higher.

* * *

I learned that it was impossible for me to expect that what was important to me would be important to others. The intensity of my dedication was performed as merely adequate on another body.

* * *

An artist stands at the foot of a stairway. A career looms above. Is it one or two steps up? How many steps to reach this destiny? This is the real challenge—to know how many steps to fulfillment. Some artists reach their goal with three steps because it rests three steps away. Others keep advancing, never knowing how much farther to go. Sometimes their goal is achieved after they are gone, by others.

* * *

One of the unfortunate things about knowledge is that, inevitably, once you've learned to play the game, the rules change.

* * *

There are times in life when you must think like a salmon: you're either going upstream or you're going nowhere.

* * *

The need for a new word to balance choreography. Dance writing and dance reading, which is the audience's role.

*** *

I've worked for years with a torn cartilage and a torn conscience, and I don't know which is worse.

*** *

Protest as I may, I know that somewhere that bad performance still exists if only in my own memory.

*** *

The most difficult times of a career are the plateaus—handling the long, flat, nowheres—the even existence—the calms.

*** *

Artificiality is spawning fish in a chlorinated pool.

*** *

Art is not "precious" in its conception, only in its sale price.

*** *

The crystal ball I use to see the future gets cloudier each year. What with the finger smudges and bits of chocolate and caramel smeared all over it, it's a wonder I can see anything at all. But what is so wonderful about this crystal ball is that it bounces. Isn't that a special gift? No matter how hard it carries me to the ground, it never stays down for long. It bounces up again and takes me with it and I go soaring with the gorgeous beast of art as it lifts me, filling me with wonder. Except I've never grown prepared for the bounces. They still jar me.

*** *

I once heard an artist say, "Success was something other people made of my life." The artist can only protest and practice the man-to-man combat of slings and arrows.

*** *

Ambition is fine, if you go in for that sort of thing. But you've got to make sure the new road you take is going onward or at least forward. But I've never trusted ambition. I've seen too many people eager to leave a destination, not knowing that they had already arrived.

163

Artists make their faith important. It is always shocking to them to discover what others deem important.

Academia is based on all the past formulas for success.

Some artists are dedicated 125 percent. They suck the extra 25 percent from others, from those around them.